PORTRAIT
OF THE
MASTER

By James F. Twyman

Foreword by Gregg Braden

FINDHORN
Press

First published in 2000
Reprinted 2001, 2004

ISBN 1-899171-43-6

Also published as a paperback under the title *The Prayer of St. Francis*
ISBN 1-899171-54-1

British Library Cataloguing-in-Publication Data.
A catalogue record for this book is available from the British Library.

Library of Congress Card Number: 00-105096

Edited by Tony Mitton and Judee Pouncey
Layout by Pam Bochel and Thierry Bogliolo
Cover illustration provided by Hermann Muller
Front cover design by Dale Vermeer

Printed and bound in the USA

Published by
Findhorn Press

305a The Park, Findhorn
Forres IV36 3TE
Scotland
Tel 01309 690582
Fax 01309 690036
e-mail info@findhornpress.com
findhornpress.com

Contents

Foreword

Once in a while, a book comes into our lives that stands apart from others in a way that is difficult to describe through words alone. The power of such a book transcends a simple summary or endorsement, and can be known only through the direct experience of the reader. *Portrait of the Master* is one of those books. Within the pages of its fifteen chapters, author and Peace Troubadour James Twyman shares his vision of a brief, yet key moment, in the life of St. Francis of Assisi. With that moment we are given insight into a possibility of such hope, creating a feeling so tangible, that its message lingers long after the cover has been closed. Inviting us to move beyond the way that we think about our world, *Portrait of the Master* teaches us how to feel peace in the trials of our everyday lives. In doing so, we become living examples of an ancient teaching, and experience the sense that, just perhaps, the power of our peace can make a difference in our world.

Almost universally, ancient texts and traditions remind us that the events of our lives are a reflection of the feeling-world within us. From this perspective, the healing of our bodies, the success of our relationships, the peace of our families, communities and nations are related in ways that we are just beginning to understand. In the language of their day, the innermost teachings of sacred orders and priesthoods passed this great secret from generation to generation, preserving the knowledge of our ability to bring peace to our world, by changing the way we feel in our bodies. Recent discoveries in quantum physics now support precisely such relationships, identifying a previously unrecognized form of energy that mirrors our feelings throughout creation in subtle, yet powerful, ways. The rich vocabulary now offered by modern science describes this relationship in a way that suggests it was both recognized, and practiced, during a time in our past; the time of Francis Bernardone—the man who became St. Francis of Assisi.

In the traditions of saints and spiritual masters, St. Francis stands alone as the most widely accepted, most visible and best known of the medieval saints. Often portrayed as an eccentric who preached to animals, dressed in rags and lived with a small band of loyal followers, the very name of St. Francis evokes the image of a man who shared his message of peace through his life of simplicity. In the absence of land and material possessions, Francis reasoned, no property boundaries could be established, nothing needed to be defended, nor could anything be taken from him. It was from this state of freedom that St. Francis based his teachings and lived his example of perpetual peace and abundance. In the simplicity of his message, miracles occurred as peasants, nobles, kings and even the pope himself were transformed in his presence.

In the summer of 1210 A.D. St. Francis made a pilgrimage to Rome for a personal audience with Innocent III, the ruler of Catholic Europe. With him, he carried a request that his teachings be recognized and endorsed by the Church. Following a mysterious dream that the Pope had during Francis' visit, his request was granted and he returned to Assisi with the blessing of the Church to found a new religious order. Through the efforts of beloved disciples such as brothers Leo, Angelo and Thomas, we are given insight into the philosophy of the merchant's son who renounced his birthright of privilege, empowered the masses through a message of personal peace, and founded the Franciscan Order of the Roman Catholic Church. Though we have copious records of his accomplishments, the fact remains that we know very little of the man who became a saint within two years of his death. What intimate thoughts did he share with those close to him? What set him apart from others of his time? Through *Portrait of the Master*, James Twyman offers insight into precisely such questions. In the informative, yet easy-to-read style that has become the hallmark of his writing, James Twyman offers a rare glimpse into a pivotal time in the life of Francis of Assisi; his journey into enemy territory during the crusades to offer his discoveries of the power of peace to the Muslim leaders. Pulling back the veils of time to a precise moment in history, Twyman offers us educated insight into the loving friendship, fears and doubts of Francis and his beloved brother, Leo, as they endure their passage into the harsh lands of the Middle East. Along the way, we listen to Francis' teachings, as Leo asks the questions of his day; questions that echo throughout each day of our lives, as well. "Explain what you mean by prayer." "Are there times more suited for prayer than others?" With answers that are as meaningful today as they were nearly eight hundred years ago, we listen as St. Francis lays the foundation for the powerful prayer of peace that we know today, The Prayer of St. Francis/Make Me An Instrument of Your Peace. Portraying the master as a very real man, with very human desires and human dilemmas, St. Francis leaps from the pages of Twyman's book into our hearts as a mortal that we can relate to, rather than a saint that we can only aspire to become.

With *Portrait of the Master*, James Twyman has written a timeless account of our own journey into the uncharted territory of life's fears, doubts and uncertainties. Through his depiction of Francis of Assisi, we are shown how the power of a simple man, with a simple message, won the respect of his peers, the Church, even his enemies, and became the most beloved of medieval saints. In the eloquence of his message, from a man who could only imagine us in his dreams, we are reminded that within each of us lives the wisdom to become an instrument of peace.

Gregg Braden
Author of *The Isaiah Effect, Walking Between the Worlds* and *Awakening to Zero Point*

THIS IS DEDICATED TO JILL

Historical background

St Francis of Assisi made three attempts to preach to the Muslims. In 1212 AD he was shipwrecked on his way to the Holy Land and had to return to Italy. A year or two later sickness forced him to abandon a journey to the Moors in Spain. In 1219 he went to Egypt where the soldiers of the Fifth Crusade were engaged in capturing Damietta in the Nile Delta. With a brother friar called Illuminato, he succeeded in entering the Muslim camp and preached to the Sultan (successor of the great Saladin and ruler of Syria and Egypt). Reportedly, the Sultan was impressed and gave him permission to visit the holy places in Palestine. However, news of disturbances among the friars in Italy forces Francis to return home.

We need not be surprised at St. Francis' use of modern terms such as 'ego'. His thought is timeless and seeks to express itself in the language most appropriate to the listener's understanding.

Chapter One

The Journey Begins

rancis had been inside the chapel of San Damiano far too long, Brother Leo thought to himself as he paced back and forth in front of the entrance, wondering what he should do. Had he broken the vow he made the day his spiritual father gave him the commission he both loved and despised? Of all the brothers in the order, why had he been chosen for such a distasteful task?

Years earlier Francis had instructed him that he must never be allowed to visit his dearest Clare alone, as if the fire of their Divine love would engulf not only them but the chapel, the town and all of Italy. He had never been uneasy about this part of his commission before, that of blocking Francis' view of Sister Clare. But now he had failed, offering no resistance at all when his brother asked him to wait by the door while they spoke in the chapel alone.

"I am your charge," Francis had said to him years earlier. "You must watch over me as if I am a child, and guard me as if I am an idiot with no understanding of the world. Most of all, dear brother, I must never be allowed to look upon her beauty, the holy and blessed Clare of God, who has given her life to Christ as an angel surrenders itself to the sky. I will remain here on earth, serving the Beloved with feet that walk and a voice that sings. But Clare, oh, she is so different from me, Brother Leo. The earth cannot hope to claim her, for the Beloved has seen fit to pull her close to Its Holy Breast and feed her as if she was the first born of life itself.

"Whenever we come here to San Damiano, you and I will stand outside the door, and you will place yourself between me and the Beloved of God, blocking my view of her. And if we talk awhile of the grace of the Almighty or the passion of the Divine, you will need remember all that we say, for as soon as the words leave my lips they will be absorbed by her grace. I could not hope to remember words that are flung so high. It is mine but to watch her shadow and know she is near me. This is all you must allow, dearest Brother, for any more than this would wound me in a way I cannot explain. I am content with the sound of her feet upon the stone step. It does more to satisfy me than all the riches of Assisi."

Things were much different for Sister Clare. She longed to look upon the humble man who had given her this new life. The shield that was Leo was like a great ocean between them, blocking the view of her spiritual lover. Years earlier, since abandoning the riches of her family in favor of the example set by her beloved Francis, she had resigned herself to the walls of this convent, hiding herself from the ordinary world within which the brothers still existed. She would leave only when

Francis called to her; her love for him was greater and more holy than any human love. And because of his promise to Francis, Leo would stand between these two lovers of God, as if they were pillars to lift him before the throne of Heaven.

Clare would always look past Leo, hoping for a glance from Francis, as if they were ancient lovers returning to the embrace of their passion. To stand between them was almost too much for Leo to bear. But for the love of God and the spirit of obedience, he did bear it. It was better for him than anything else he could imagine, for he was sure that no greater love existed in all the world than that love between Francis and Clare.

But not on this day, Leo thought to himself, the sound of his feet echoing off the high stone wall of the convent. His mind was so concentrated on what he had allowed that he forgot to stop and listen to the birds that sang in the nearby olive trees. This was a rare thing indeed, for Leo loved the birds of Assisi, the way they played and gathered their tiny morsels of food. He often compared the brothers to these wondrous creatures of God, so simple and content with the graces they received, and it was this, more than anything, which drew him to become a Franciscan. He was just a child when Francis left behind his father's wealth and adopted the cloak of a poor beggar. And when the town reviled him and the children flung stones at him, even then Leo wondered what it would be like to live in such freedom, to cast away the fruitless pandering of mundane life and abandon one's self to the beatific embrace of the Divine. He was one of the first to recognize the holiness of Francis' decision, and when he was able, just days after he turned seventeen years, he left his own father and everything he represented, and began to follow the "King of Beggars".

Leo's love of nature and the simplicity of his new life made him strive for a way to express his passion. Even as a child he would sketch what he saw, drawn as he was to the natural world and the creatures of God. He would often hide his crudely stitched pad beneath his cloak and steal away to the hills that surrounded Assisi. Once there Leo would gaze deep into his own life, pulling from that reservoir a rich collection of images and lights, the dark hues and subtle shades that blended so naturally with what he saw all around himself. The pad was filled with drawings of the birds and the animals that wandered around him as if he belonged there. It was only natural, then, for him to follow the example set by Francis, the saint who was one with nature. They were so much alike, and this, more than anything, was the reason Leo was assigned the task of chronicling the life of the brothers through art.

Until then Francis had never allowed his image to be drawn or recorded in any way. Was it the humble nature of the man that formed him so, or was there something deeper that no one else could see or perceive? Whatever the reason, Leo was overjoyed when he heard that Francis had changed his mind in this regard. Leo's role of blocking Francis' view of the holy Clare seemed over, and he was at last given permission to draw a portrait of the master.

"The founder of our order is about to leave on one of his famous journeys," the brother superior had told him days earlier, "and I want you, Brother Leo, to accompany him, and in doing so to capture his likeness on your pad. No one knows where he is off to, but there is a seriousness in his eye that I have never seen before. That is what I want you to capture in your drawing, the deep penetration of his gaze when he considers what only a saint can perceive. The portrait you produce will be the official representation of the future saint, so pray to the Blessed Mother that she may guide your hand."

"Brother, until now it has been mine to stand between the saint you speak of and his holy counterpart, Sister Clare," Leo said to his superior. "Whenever he leaves for the blessed chapel of San Damiano, I am called upon to render this service, and for the love of my vow to holy obedience I have served willingly. I have always remained silent in my desire to capture his blessed likeness, though I have secretly longed for the chance. Until now I have been but his shield and a dagger for his heart. What has suddenly changed that my desire would now be fulfilled?"

"Brother Francis himself has asked it," the man said. "I do not know why, but something has changed in his countenance. This mission he is off to fulfill is of some critical importance, and that is all I know of it. He also told me that he has something to teach you. He said that you would understand."

Leo thought about this for a moment, wondering what the brother could mean. Then he remembered something he said to Francis months earlier, a question regarding the use of prayer in the soul's ascension to the Divine. Prayer was so important to the vocation of the brothers, and Leo knew that there was a deeper rhythm that only Francis understood. It was this knowledge that Leo wanted for himself. More than anything, Leo wanted to see through the eyes of holiness, to perceive the beatific vision with a full and open heart. Perhaps this is what the brother superior was referring to.

"Go to him, then," Leo was told. "Make yourself known to the poorest man in Assisi, and the richest. Whatever it is you desire, may it be granted to you through the mercy of the Divine. And when you return from this sacred journey, bring with you the portrait we desire, that we may remember his face for many generations."

eo continued pacing back and forth in front of the chapel while he remembered these things. Another moment and his resolve would surely have been broken. Just when he determined that he should burst into the chapel and steal Francis from the embrace of their togetherness, Francis appeared in the entrance with Clare directly behind him. They stood there for a moment without words, absorbing the last rays of their spiritual union and light. Then Clare turned and closed the door, returning to her cloister.

Leo was afraid to interrupt Francis' aloneness. A great sadness flowed from him, and Leo watched it rise like a cloud above the Italian countryside. And just as clouds are prone to do in Assisi, it came with a fury, then left. Leo then felt a clarity in his brother which was not present before, and as they walked down the path that led away from San Damiano, that clarity increased as their pace did quicken.

"We are off to perform a mission of peace, Brother Leo. You have not failed in your vows, but fulfilled them. Before I could leave I needed to consult her, to pull from within her the will of the Divine. And now that I have looked into her eyes and have seen the pulse of my own longing, now we can go. It is time for us to fulfill the truest task we can be given to fulfill."

"But where are we going?" Leo asked as he struggled to keep up with Francis.

"We are going to fulfill the admonishment of Christ," Francis said. "We have been told to love our enemies and to bless those who curse us. This law is higher than anything made by man, and must be considered our most sacred task. Even if the highest human authorities ask me to refuse this call, I must close my ears to them. I am true only to the Divine, and it is to God that I will answer for this."

"Will you tell me where we are going?" Leo's plea was more heartfelt than before and Francis suddenly felt obliged to answer him.

"You and I, Leo, are leaving immediately for the Crusades. We will not stop to gather anything for this journey but will go with empty hands and full hearts. The other brothers know nothing of this trip, for to tell them would put them in great danger. You see, we are not going to comfort the Christians, but to sing the message of peace to the Muslims. I intend to travel across enemy lines and make my way to the Sultan himself, and express however I can the true message of Christ. When I do, I am sure he will understand and will stop this terrible war. If not, then I will die a martyr, and will gladly accept this sentence. Either way I am doing what I must, and Clare agrees."

Leo stood with his feet rooted in the earth, unable to move. Was he hearing correctly? In all the years he had been with him, he had never heard Francis speak so resolutely. But this was insane. He couldn't really mean what he said, for it was suicide. The Crusades had been raging for many years and thousands of Christian soldiers had given their lives to protect the Church. Why would a simple monk want to cross into this hell thinking that he could succeed where everyone else had failed, even if he was a saint?

"You must forgive me, Leo, for I have neglected you. You have been my companion for many years and have fulfilled your role perfectly. But I cannot allow you to come with me across the enemy lines. This is my path and I cannot ask anyone to follow. I cannot even ask you to accompany me as I prepare for this journey for there may be grave consequences to anyone who assists me."

"What kind of consequences?" Leo asked him.

"Yesterday I received a message from His Holiness the Pope ordering me not to travel to Syria to see the Sultan. He said that if I refuse and disobey him I will be excommunicated from the Church. He pleaded with me not to throw away everything I have worked so hard to achieve. But I believe that to turn away from the Muslims is to abandon the very foundation of our order, and Christ himself. They are children of God just as we are, and this war over religion must end. If it takes my being excommunicated then I will accept that. But I cannot ask the same of you."

Leo stood there for a very long time looking into the eyes of his brother. What would he say? He began to experience a strange mix of fear and courage, half of him wanting to follow and the other half unable to. And yet he was not at all surprised by the path Francis had decided to take. He had been talking about nothing else for weeks, preaching day and night about peace and the call of Christ to not resist evil. And then he would leave for long days and nights of prayer, going high into the hills of Mount Subasio where he could be alone in his cave. Was this what he was laying before God, this plan of disobedience and redemption? It was no small thing for Francis to go against Rome, so attached was he to the successor of St. Peter. Leo understood the import of this decision, and did not hesitate to reveal himself.

"I will not leave you," he said. "Brother Francis, I could never let you go alone into this peril. I am your companion and would forsake everything to be at your side, even if it means that I too am excommunicated."

"Brother Leo, I cannot allow you to cross the border with me. If it is your wish, you can travel with me that far, and I will welcome your company. But when we come to the area occupied by the Muslims, I will turn you back. You will then tell the other brothers of my decision, and, God willing, I will return to them."

"There is one thing I must ask," Brother Leo said to him. "No… there are two things I must ask of you. I have been told of your desire to let me capture your likeness on my pad. You know how long I have desired this, and I am so grateful. I ask, then, that you let me conduct this affair without your knowledge. In other words, I will draw when you are not aware, when you are absorbed in some other activity. In this way I will capture the essence of your life as you live it, not posed and staged, but natural.

"The second thing I ask is that you teach me the true meaning of peace and prayer. I have listened to you for years, all the ways you honor and express the holy teachings, but it is so hard for me to understand. I ask that, as we travel forward on this path, you take the time to explain your deeper understanding of the 'Peace that surpasseth understanding.' If you will do these things I will be so very grateful, and will follow you anywhere. I will also draw a portrait that will rival the works of the masters."

Francis reached out and touched Leo's face. "I will honor both of your requests. Do not show me your drawing until you are finished. It may be too much for me to bear otherwise. And I will teach you everything I know about the Peace of God, Brother Leo. It will be good to remind myself as I approach this test of faith."

And this is how the journey began. Neither one knew what lay ahead, but Brother Leo had what he wanted. It would be weeks before they would approach the battlefield, weeks with the undivided attention of a saint. What more could Leo ask for? At that moment nothing else mattered to him.

Chapter Two

The Art of Prayer

eo's feet were tired and he desperately needed to rest. "Please, Francis, let us stop here for just a moment. We have been walking for hours and your pace quickens with each step. It feels as if I am doing penance just trying to keep up with you."

Francis looked back at Leo, obviously unaware of his friend's discomfort. "Forgive me, my brother," he said as he walked back to where Leo stood exhausted. "My mind is filled with the teachings of our Blessed Lord, the eloquent and important way he taught us about the Peace of God, or what you yourself called, the 'peace that surpasseth understanding'. It saddens me to think how few people consider the depth of his words, even though he was most clear on the subject. It is easier to accept the ideas and teachings that fit neatly into one's present beliefs, but ignore the more subtle and essential lessons that challenge us to change.

"You see, Brother Leo, before we can accept the true meaning of peace, a transformation is required which shakes the very foundation of our lives. This transformation requires that we lay aside all the concepts and beliefs we presently hold, and accept a new vision offered by the Mind of the Beloved. If we think we already have the answer, if we are hard in our ways and closed in our thoughts, then we cannot hear the Voice for God which whispers its secrets softly into our ear. For most it is a confronting task they will never face. But it is in truth the greatest victory one can achieve as we ascend toward the throne of the Beloved."

"But if this change makes clear the Mind and the Will of God, why do we hesitate at all?" Brother Leo asked. "Isn't this our greatest desire, to be in that Mind and to know the secrets of the Divine?"

"The threshing floor of God is a marvelous place to the one who happily submits to the Will of God, just as you have described, Brother. But to the one who clings to the world, it is a dreadful, fearful thing. When laid upon the cutting board of the Divine, we are asked to submit to the gentle hands of God which knead and mold us according to the vision of holiness. If we are pliant and submit to this test, then we are made into holy bread, and consecrated as holy wine, which in turn nourish the whole world. But if we resist, if we cower in fear before the Hand of God, then we remain hard and unyielding, like a useless crust that is thrown into the fire. It is our fear of what we can become which chains us to these forms. And in order to avoid the transformation of love, we cling to what we think we know, rather than accept the clearer vision that could be ours."

"You speak of transformation and the transmutation of our desires into the Will of God," Leo said. "It sounds as if our natural state is not at all inclined toward the peace you describe."

"Oh, it's just the opposite, my dearest brother. It is in our natural state that we come closest to discovering the reality of peace, the pulse of Divine Light that most truly defines us. But we have piled inestimable layers of false, unnatural beliefs upon that holy altar, so that it is now a darkened memory, a lost and forgotten vestige of the reality it reflects. The natural bend of the shadowy mind is toward conflict, as you yourself have seen. The further we move from the natural position of harmony and peace, the more we see war and conflict as real solutions. We then project that vision into the world and draw from that world all the things that correspond to and justify this version of reality.

"But if the foundation of that reality is false, Brother Leo, then everything that comes from it is false as well. One cannot preserve certain elements of what is inherently false and hope they transfer to the experience of what is true. Do you understand? What is false must be completely abandoned and a new vision accepted, one that resonates with the Mind of God, from which all reality springs. Until then we are competing with that Mind, and such a competition is the essence of vanity."

Brother Leo looked at Francis with confused and lost eyes. He tried desperately to grasp everything he heard, but he was a simple man and thought in simple ways. Francis, in his great compassion, understood immediately and asked Leo to sit down with him at the side of the road.

"There was once a man who owned a very large plot of land which he inherited from a distant relative. Because he was not accustomed to modern methods of farming, he employed the help of a gentleman he met one evening who said he could teach him what he needed to know to produce an abundant harvest. Unknown to the man who inherited the land, this rugged gentleman was in truth a thief who intended to steal his money with no return at all. The thief filled a cloth sack with small metal beads claiming they were the most fertile seeds in the entire country. He then said he would gladly sell these magic seeds to the farmer for a healthy sum, and that his investment would make him the richest man for many miles.

"Well, the farmer was so interested in making a profit from his inheritance that he paid the thief, who then left that area with his pockets overflowing with money, afraid he would soon be discovered as a fraud. The farmer, in the meantime, immediately planted the beads and waited to reap the enormous harvest he was promised. Months went without a single sprout. Though the ground itself was fertile and rich with life, the metal beads refused to produce life, for they were themselves dead and lifeless. The man soon realized his misfortune and waited until the next season.

"Winter came and the ground slept. When spring finally came, the farmer heard a still, quiet voice within him that said, 'Do not plant a single seed this year, but wait patiently for the harvest that is already yours.' Since he was still ignorant of the ways of the earth he decided to heed the advice and he did not lift a finger all season. Summer came and he discovered, to his utter amazement, that the voice was right. A marvelous crop rose from the earth and he was soon richer than he ever could have imagined."

"I think I understand your story," Brother Leo said, "but please explain to me how it relates to what you were saying before."

"Each one of us enters a world fertile with possibilities," Francis explained. "When we are born, we are like a rich piece of land which has the potential to produce an enormous harvest, or become a parched desert through misuse. And since we are new to this venture, we search for someone to guide us and help us use our inheritance wisely. It is critical that we choose a guide who is looking out for our best interest, otherwise we will be robbed and have to wait for the next season.

"There are two voices or guides we constantly choose between," he continued. "The first is the one who guides us toward truth, into the natural rhythms of a life that reveals our true nature. The second guide tricks us into believing that there is a shortcut to achieving our goal. This one is like the thief who filled the sack with metal beads claiming they were magic seeds. If the farmer had learned to trust his intuition, that which was inherently true within him, he would have been led along naturally and would have certainly been successful.

"Instead he decided to trust the thief. The thief believes he knows a better way, that he can bypass the natural route and arrive at the goal quicker and with greater gain. What he does not realize is that the true seeds were already planted in the farmer's lot long before he inherited the land. If he had been patient and waited for the proper season of growth, he would have discovered that a bountiful harvest was already his. But in his rush toward wealth, he disrupted the seeds that slept beneath the ground, setting them back an entire season.

The metal beads could not grow, for they were dead and useless things."

"But then the next season came and the true seeds did sprout," Leo said as if he suddenly understood the parable.

"This final part of the story illustrates the compassion of God, who never steals the inheritance which is rightfully ours. The harvest is a gift, and it is a gift that can never be lost. We can delay our enjoyment of God's bounty, but we can never throw it away forever. Even the most sinful among us who squanders the gifts so generously bestowed by the Beloved, even that person will sleep as did the earth in our story, only to be reborn again to wait upon the Lord. This is the mercy our Savior spoke of when he walked among us. This was the meaning of his most holy parables. And it is the secret to discovering the generous portion bestowed upon each and every single one of us today."

"I understand," Leo said as he jumped up from his seat. "The Peace of God is already within us. To worry about and force that which is already present is to disrupt the natural flow of creation. That is what the mystic meant who said 'Wait patiently upon the Lord.' To over-anticipate the gifts of God is to believe they are not already there, and this anxiousness cuts off the flow of energy that would otherwise nurture and sustain that gift. When we wait in earnest longing, certain of the Beloved's promise, then we enjoy the fruit of the seeds which were planted within us when we were created."

"You understand more than you let on, my dear brother," Francis said as he stood up and put his arm around Leo. "The mysteries of the peace you seek are nearly yours."

"It is easy to understand when you tell me simple stories. It gives my mind something to wrap itself around."

"Then I will tell you another." Francis took Leo by the arm and they began walking down the road again. "There was another farmer in a different country who had a field very much like the man in our first story. This farmer had tried every kind of plant and seed but failed to grow a suitable crop season after season. One day he heard a knock on his door and when he went to answer, he saw a holy man from the mountain standing in front of him. Now this holy man was famous throughout that region and the farmer was overjoyed to have such an honored guest in his home.

"But the holy man would not enter the house. He stood outside the door and held out a velvet bag filled with seeds, telling the farmer in a low, serious voice that it came from an ancient temple renowned for its wisdom and power. The seeds had been kept inside a golden urn for hundreds of years and were therefore dry and lifeless. He then told the farmer that they possessed magical powers that when unleashed would produce the greatest harvest known to humanity. The holy man had decided to give the seeds to the farmer as a gift. They would sprout only if he discovered the secret that would reveal their power. Otherwise, they would be of no value to him at all."

"Did he ever discover the secret?" Leo asked, clearly caught up in the story.

"For many weeks he studied magic formulas and read every book he could find. He cast spells on the seeds, recited words from ancient and forgotten lands. But the seeds did not change. They remained as dead as the day the holy man gave them to him. The farmer was heartbroken, for he believed everything the holy man had said. He decided that he was a failure in this as in everything.

"Then one day something very unexpected happened. The farmer had set a glass of water next to the velvet bag and when he turned away the water spilled onto the table and the bag was drenched. At first he thought nothing of this accident, but several days later he noticed that the bag was larger than before. He opened the velvet bag and discovered to his amazement that the seeds had sprouted. He poured them onto the table and screamed with delight. When harvest time came that farmer produced the most abundant crop in that country."

"You must explain this one to me, Francis. As in your last story, I believe the seed represents the gifts of God. But what is the significance of the water which unleashed the seeds' power?"

"Just as you said, Brother Leo, each one of us receives from our Divine Parent gifts that are bestowed freely and with joy. But if we do not use those gifts wisely, they grow old and dry, as if they were dead. But no matter how much time goes by, no matter how much we neglect the seed of our Divinity, there is a magical secret which has the power to bring it back to life, unleashing its power. When we discover that secret, then apply it, we begin to grow spiritually, and we achieve Divine riches beyond our imagination."

"And what is that secret?"

"This is how I will keep my promise to you, Brother Leo. I will teach you about that secret, for it is the simplest, most holy thing you can set before you. That is how you will learn the deeper meaning of peace. This secret will be the water that enlivens your soul, bringing back to life the bountiful gifts that have been yours since the beginning of time. Over the course of our journey, I will teach you the mysteries of that secret, and the seed of your life will sprout, then produce an abundant harvest. Then you will know everything that I know, and you will understand the Divine pulse in the same way that I understand it. That is the gift I will give you, Brother Leo. It is all I can ever truly offer."

"Please tell me, then, what is the secret, the water that enlivens the dry and lifeless seed within us?"

"It is so simple, Leo. It is prayer. Prayer is the water that brings the soul back to life. And I will teach you how to pray. Then you will be as rich as the farmer in our story. Each day of our journey together I will give you a prayer to focus your mind on. Each prayer will be like a code that may elude your mind, but enliven your heart. When we arrive at the Crusades, you will have everything you need to experience the true meaning of prayer. Then the foundation of reality will not seem so far away, my dear brother, but will appear before you, in you and all around you. You are that foundation, so this prayer will bring you back to you. Then I will leave you and go on to the Sultan."

Chapter Three

"Lord, make me an instrument of your peace"

t was nearly evening and the two men had been walking for hours. Leo sauntered along behind Francis trying to consider and absorb everything he had learned during that first day. He felt as if he was walking on air, so overjoyed was he to have this time alone with the famous saint. He was content to listen and learn, confident that he would soon grasp the very essence of peace.

"Brother Leo, I would like to talk to you more about prayer," Francis said as he suddenly stopped and spun around. "I told you earlier that it is the magical ingredient that inspires the soul and ignites the true experience of peace. For a soul who has been hardened by hatred and despair, or for the one whose life is ruled by fear and has forgotten how to love, prayer is like an ointment that soothes and resurrects, bringing back to life that which seemed dead and alone."

"Explain to me what you mean by prayer," Leo said. "It seems that there are so many ways to open to God."

"Prayer is surrender, Brother Leo. It is stepping back into the arms of the Divine and melting into the embrace of the Beloved. There are so many ways to pray, but it this merging that is important. To ask God to provide something you think you do not have is the lowest level of prayer. To open the soul to the brilliance of eternity, drinking in the light of God as if it were a fountain, this is the highest. It is the wordless prayer that God cannot ignore, because it unites the soul with the Divine current from which all life flows. There are also prayers that use words and concepts, and they are not less than wordless prayer. The power of our prayer is born upon the wings of our intent, and nothing else. It is there we must turn if we are to judge the worth of our song to God. When our intention is love, then prayer is the path that leads us to the throne of our true home."

"When we recite the prayers of the ancients are we further from God than when we speak from our hearts?"

"Prayer is never contained by the words we speak, my brother, but by the devotion within which we enfold our words. Without this love, no matter how beautiful the prayer, it is empty and lifeless. It was this energy the Apostle Paul spoke of when he said that without love we are like clanging symbols. When we pray from our hearts, the ether of our love attaches itself to our prayer and our prayer is carried by the wings of angels to the altar of the Divine. Without love, our prayers are like lead weights which are too heavy for the angels to carry. They lie upon the ground and are forgotten, never once feeling the sharp wind of the Heavenly sky."

Leo looked in front of them and saw a man pulling a cart filled with wood toward a nearby village. Though the cart appeared heavy and full, the man whistled a happy tune as he walked, and Leo wondered how the man's mood could remain so light while pulling such a massive load.

"Look at that man," Francis said to him. "You and I together would not be able to pull that cart as well as he. And yet there he is, happy and whistling a song, totally unaware of his task, but fulfilling it with love. It would be reasonable for him to curse the load, to bemoan his arduous task and dream of the hour when he leaves it behind. I tell you that his song is his prayer, and the weight of his cart is not at all related to the delight he feels. Were it not for the song, he would curse a load half that size. It is his intent that lightens his way, not his strength. Remove that intent and the cart would fasten itself to the earth. His prayer aligns him with energies he is completely unaware of, but which serve to unite him to the spirits of the earth and sky."

"Are there times which are more suited for prayer than others?" Leo asked.

"If there were, then that man would do better to save his song for another time and another place. It is like asking if there are times more suited for breathing. Prayer is the act of being conscious of the breath of God that flows through and around us every instant of our lives. Would that Divine breath forget us for even an instant? The practice of prayer, then, is to become aware of the Awareness of God. Each breath we breathe, every thought we think, becomes an act of prayer, for we cannot be separated from that breath except in our dreams."

Francis and Leo followed the man and soon arrived in the village. They watched as he parked the cart in a shed, then walked to the door of a nearby house. A small child opened the door and threw her arms around her father who then went inside. The two men stood there and watched the scene with great joy, then walked on to beg for their evening meal.

As they walked toward the center of the village, they saw a man leaning against a stone wall playing a small wooden flute. The music he played was sweet and melodic and Francis began to dance happily in the street. Within minutes a crowd gathered to watch the strange but interesting way he swayed to the music, back and forth, leaping in the air with his arms outstretched. Leo was embarrassed and stood to the side watching. Then he heard a woman who was standing near him say that she recognized the strange beggar. A debate began in the crowd as to whether this was the 'Saint from Assisi,' the famous Brother Francis who had so inspired Italy and all of Europe. The man playing the flute was overjoyed to have such an appreciative audience, and when Francis stopped dancing, everyone in the crowd, which had by then grown to over fifty, began to applaud wildly. Even the man leaning against the stone wall showed his gratitude and clapped his huge hands together.

Though Francis was nearly out of breath, he launched into one of the impromptu sermons he was famous for. He looked to the sky and stretched his arms out like a giant bird, the sleeves of his habit falling down and giving the impression of wings.

"Oh, Lord, make me an instrument of your peace," he prayed in a loud and penetrating voice. "Carve me into a flute that is placed to your Divine lips, and fill me with the breath of your spirit. Wrap your fingers around my soul and cover the holes of my life. Make of me a song to the Beloved, a hymn to the holiness of your Divine and gracious love. Teach me what it means to surrender to the rhythm of your dance, Beloved One. Destroy the empty vessel of my vanity, and fill me with your sacred wine. Let me drink until I am overcome by your love, then hold me straight that I may fall into your open arms.

"Oh, Lord, teach me to become an instrument of your grace. Open my heart and let your love flow into me like a river of refreshment. Then place my mouth against your own that I may taste the sweetness of your lips, and gulp the full measure of your holy breath. Let your music resound in my heart and so overwhelm me that I can no longer contain myself. Then let me dance to the rhythmic pounding of our joined hearts, the celestial pulse without which I cannot survive.

"Lord, make me an instrument of your passion. Stir the depths of my spirit and show me what it feels like to go mad from loving you. Let my heart scream from the pain of too much tenderness, and be wounded by the arrow of your sharp and penetrating gaze. Lock me inside your bedchamber and force me to wait upon your embrace. And when daylight fades and you come to me at last, beckon me with your eyes and I will fall into you, just as a river merges with the sea or as the earth wraps itself around the roots of a mighty tree."

The crowd was so overwhelmed by the beauty of his words that many of the women fell to their knees and the men began to pray aloud. They gathered around the saint and asked him to bless them. And Francis looked into their eyes and told them that they were already blessed by the Lord. For over an hour he walked among the people, praying and telling them of the love of God. Then they were gone and Leo stood before his brother, and they embraced.

"Thank you for letting me attend to you in this way," Leo said to Francis. "I am probably the richest man in Umbria, though I am still a beggar for God."

"The riches of God have nothing to do with money, Brother Leo. We have within us a source of abundance that the world cannot understand. Yet few of us will ever discover the origin of that wealth because we tend to look outside ourselves and believe we can only be satisfied by worldly riches. The treasure we seek is within our hearts, dearest brother. It is there that we must dig, beneath the desires and the appetite of the ego. When we have conquered those demons, then the mine breaks open and the gold spills at our feet. We then discover the true meaning of wealth, which is the same as grace, which is the same as love."

A short time later Francis and Leo sat together in a large pile of hay, a suitable bed for two travelers. They had already eaten the bread and the cheese they begged from a kind woman they met in the village, and they were both tired from a long day of walking. Leo thought about the prayer Francis shared with the crowd. It was not unusual for Francis to express himself so eloquently, but there was something he said that struck Leo in a new way.

"Francis, you spoke tonight about becoming an instrument of peace. The man who played the flute was surely the inspiration of this prayer, but I was hoping you would explain it further."

"I want you to closely consider the first line from that prayer, Leo. Let this be the prayer you focus on in your dreams: 'Lord, make me an instrument of your peace.' Two of these words are more important than all the others— they are 'instrument' and 'your.' Let us begin with the word 'instrument.' Like the flute that was played by the man leaning against the stone wall, an instrument cannot play itself. It must surrender to the musician in order to be played. It may think that its own breath can produce the sound it desires, but no music comes from it at all, except in its imagination. But this imagination would try to deceive truth, and change the rules of reality. This is the greatest offense one can imagine, for who can change the Holy Will of God?

"Likewise, each one of us is called to be an instrument of peace. And yet it is only when we surrender to the Divine current within that we are played, just like the flute. Otherwise we are as silent as a reed, anticipating sound and music, imagining the flow of wisdom and insight that leads us nowhere. Until we realize the futility of trying to play ourselves, we are like an instrument that sits in the corner of the room. It is soon forgotten by everyone in the house.

"And then we come to the next word. 'Make me an instrument of your peace.' As I said to you earlier, it is vanity to think that we know the ways of Divine Grace. As long as we find ourselves in this state of transgression, we cannot understand the true meaning of peace. It is not our definition of peace we seek, but God's. True peace is not a definition at all, but an experience that transcends all definitions. Once we have surrendered to the Divine current that exists within us, then opened ourselves to a new vision of holiness, that experience caves in all around us, and we are suddenly entombed within the reality we seek.

It is a tomb that brings us to life, Brother Leo, not death. It is like the tomb of our Lord who saw the futility of death, then rose to eternity. Likewise, we too will experience the futility of our ego and rise to a life that exists beyond our hollow definition."

"I understand, Brother Francis. We are all called to surrender to God, to be made as instruments of Divine Peace. It is only when we release our definitions of what we think peace is that the reality of peace is given to us. And then we are asked to extend that gift, freely, just as it was freely given to us. This is the path we follow when we liberate our will and surrender to the Divinity which is the foundation of our existence."

"Brother Leo, you will soon be teaching me. I am filled with gratitude to have a companion such as you. Let us now sleep and pray the Lord teach us in our dreams."

And with that, the men covered themselves with hay and fell asleep.

Chapter Four

"Where there is hatred, let me bring love"

he next morning Francis and Leo rose at dawn and, while kneeling to face the rising sun, they began the day in prayer. Leo brushed the hay from his habit and tried desperately to clear his vision, rubbing his eyes as if he were still dreaming. Francis, meanwhile, opened his arms and began to pray in a loud voice.

"Oh, Lord, we greet the Sun which rises in the East and illumines our soul. You, holy Brother, who warm the earth making all things grow, teach us what it means to open ourselves to your radiance, pulling aside the curtains that hide our fear. Then will we see for the first time the truth which you behold, the Light that lives within our hearts not unlike your own. You look down upon us as if we are your children, and you draw all creatures into your warm embrace. And now, rising as they do, we greet this new day, asking it to draw us close to the Heavens which support and claim you even now. Teach us how to give everything we have, so that when night falls and we retire, you will clear the path for your most holy Sister, the Moon. She sleeps now, the gentle lover that follows your path. Make clear her way, dear Brother, that we may rejoice when lights fade and we sleep again in her open arms. Then will our dreams be as yours, filled with the Light that transcends the shadows of our forgotten dreams, embraced forever by our Beloved God."

Then Francis looked over at Leo and said, "I trust you slept well in your bed of hay, Brother Leo."

"There were times when I thought it was made of the softest feathers in Italy," Leo said smiling. "It reminds me of when I first joined you many years ago. My heart was so filled with love that even a stone felt soft to me then."

"I remember nights when we did sleep on slabs of stone," Francis laughed. "And even then we sang of our great wealth, though our bellies were often empty. We could see the candles flickering from every bedroom in Assisi, but our simplicity made us feel like we were more blessed than they. It is good to remember those days, my dear brother. And it is good to share this journey with you."

"I have a question I would like to ask you, Brother Francis," Leo said as he stood up. "When we arrive in Syria and stand before the Sultan, what will you say to him? It is so hard to imagine such a thing as this, but I do love to wonder about that day. I have known you for... so many years now, and I have felt your rapture when possessed by the spirit of the Beloved. But this is so different from those times. These men seek to destroy the defenders of our faith, clashing with them sword to sword. And yet we will enter their towns with no sword at all, save the sword of love and the shield of compassion."

Francis looked confused for a moment, as if he wasn't sure what he would do. He stood up from the ground and took hold of Leo's shoulders, saying: "My dearest brother, I am sorry if you didn't understand my words when we began our journey, but I cannot allow you to follow me to this uncertain destiny. I must travel to the Sultan alone, and die if it is God's will. And yet, in spite of this, my heart is overflowing with the wealth I will bestow upon him. The truth I have found must be his as well, for we are all the same in the eyes of our Lord. But you will not be at my side when the moment of this disclosure arrives. You will be on your way back to the brothers we love, holding your portrait beneath your arm."

"I do remember what you said to me, but I insist that I be allowed to continue. You have been more than a brother to me, but a father and a mother too, and you have borne for me a whole family to love. And now that we are here together, what sense does it make for me to follow you and then turn back when you need me most? I am not afraid of what might transpire. I am more afraid of how I will feel if I hear of your fate and know that I was not there for you."

Francis began to walk back in the direction of the village they had visited the day before. Leo hurried to catch up, wondering about this sudden shift.

"Where are we going, Brother Francis?"

"You believe that the adventure we seek is at the hands of the Muslims, and so you miss the adventure of the moment," Francis said. "Follow me back into this town and we will seek an answer. It is not mine to hold you from your destiny. There are signs around every corner that will lead us in the right direction. Let us seek those signs today, and thereby know the path." Then Francis stopped and looked into Leo's eyes. "I have promised to teach you the true meaning of peace, my brother. She is a mysterious lover who whispers Her secrets softly into your ear. You must have the will to abandon your earthly ears that you may hear Her voice. If She desires your presence, then you may continue with me as far as you choose. But if you're deaf to Her words, then we will stick to our original plan, and you will return to Assisi without me."

"Yes, I agree," Leo said to him. "I want to hear that sound more than anything in this world. Sometimes I feel it echoing deep in my heart, but when I finally tune my ear to the sound of Her voice, it is gone. Help me, dear brother, to quicken this sense that I may capture this prize, then we will answer Her Will with obedient steps."

"And what is it you would learn from Her, if you had this sense?" Francis asked.

"I would learn about love. I would seek the key that would unlock any door, the aroma that draws every soul into the rapture of Her grace. What could I hope to know that love would not reveal to me, if I would but answer its call?"

Francis was a few steps ahead of Leo and he seemed anxious to return to the village they had left. "Then we will seek that love today," Francis said without turning around. "We will seek Her voice through everyone we meet, diving into the mystery of love as if it were an ocean. And let this be your prayer, the holy thought that will satisfy your seeking, 'Where there is hatred let me bring love.' Surely the people of this place can offer you the lesson you desire, each one according to their own experience of love. "

And as they walked, they came upon a small boy who was running toward them. Francis stopped the child and asked, "Young boy, you who run without the staggering weight of adulthood, tell us what you know of love."

The boy stopped and thought for a moment, then looked at the two men and said: "Love is like a giant tree which I climb to the highest branch. And when I sit at the top of that tree I do not need to worry about falling, for even the wind that blows realizes I am safe within its arms. Yes, even if I were to swing back and forth from one branch to another, still would I feel safe, for I know that the tree is my friend."

They continued to walk until they saw an old woman who was gathering wood at the side of the road. Her arms were nearly filled with the small scraps she found, and when Francis asked her the same question about love, she said to him:

"Love is hard work. It does what it is told and hastens to obey the commands of the soul. It does not flash from person to person, but holds very still in the place it has been asked to live. If it were to move from that place, then an empty space would be created and loneliness would rush into the house. Yes, love is like my back which cracks and breaks, but still it bends forward, never once revealing its pain."

By then Francis and Leo were back in the village and they walked toward a fountain near a busy market square. There were many merchant carts in this place filled with a great variety of food, and the people swarmed about like bees gathering honey from every flower they saw. Francis noticed a man selling vegetables and he walked up to him, saying:

"Tell me sir, you who sell what the earth has given you, how would you define love?"

And the man stepped away from his cart so Francis could hear him above the noise of the market, and he said: "Love is like a field. It requires great care to profit from the gifts it would give. Sometimes one plants a seed in the ground but the birds find it before it has the chance to take root, so I build a wooden man that stands in the field day and night to confuse the birds. And then the seed begins to grow and weeds sprout next to the intended crop, so I get down on my knees and I separate them one by one, pulling the weeds from the earth and leaving the good plants to grow. And when it is time for the harvest, I call my sons to stand at my side that we may gather the food we sell here in this market. Yes, love is like the produce you see in my cart. It is the result of months of attention and labor, and yet it fills and nurtures our bodies that we may continue this work."

Then Francis saw a priest who was walking with his eyes locked on some holy text. He stopped the priest in the street and said: "Monsignor, you who speak to God and whose hands administer the blessed sacraments, tell me what lies behind these rituals and ancient rites. Tell me what you know of love."

And the priest stopped walking and closed his book. Then he looked over the houses that lined the square and pointed in the direction of the church, saying: "Look there if you choose to understand love. There is nothing at all beyond these rites. Everything we know has been taught to us by Holy Mother Church. It is her voice we follow, not our own. We know only that which has been revealed through her representatives here on earth, the bishops and the priests. When there is a question or a doubt, a person needs to set their attention upon the altar where truth is revealed. Yes, they must trust what has always been taught and not venture into the swamp where their discernment fails them."

A politician then passed the two men and Francis stopped him.

"Excuse me, sire, you who follow the law that dictates the righteous path we need to walk, what can you tell me about the meaning of love?"

And the politician stopped what he was doing and seized the opportunity to express his views, saying: "It is the one who follows the law that understands the true meaning of love. We live together but we walk a solitary path, lost in the dreams given to us by our parents, and they by their own. But we are not alone, are we? There are rules to follow and laws to obey. How can I love these others while I disregard the commonality of our shared dream? Why, I would not be a servant at all but a thief who claims one thing but does another."

"But I do not understand," Leo said to him. "What then is love from your perspective?"

"Oh, you seek to trap me and force me to straighten the winding path of my words?" the politician said as he began to walk away. "No, I cannot allow this at all. To make sense of these things would lessen my appreciation of love, not increase it."

Francis and Leo laughed quietly to themselves, not at all sure what to think of the man. And as they laughed, a young woman brushed up against Francis, so he stopped her and asked: "Describe for me, if you will, your vision of love. How would you define this wondrous state?"

The girl thought for a moment, pressing one finger of her delicate hand against her cheek, then smiled and answered: "Love is like a strong man whose eyes are tender and meek. He knows when it is time to use his strength, but when I approach his side his hand reaches for mine with the sensitivity of a dove. If I am confronted by one who proposes to do me harm, then he stands tall and is ready to fight. But when we are alone, he melts into my arms and becomes like a child again. Yes, this is what love is like. On the outside it appears hard and formidable, but when the armor is removed, it is soft and yielding, like a rose that pricks the hurried passer-by but leans forward to be enjoyed by the lover who appreciates its scent."

Then they saw a woman with a baby in her arms, and they approached her with the same question. "Tell us about love," Francis said to her. "Translate for us now what this child knows in his heart, and which you surely understand as well."

The woman held the baby so Francis and Leo could see his face, then she said to them: "Look into the eyes of this child and you will understand the true meaning of love. There is an innocence in this one which the world will soon rob, but for now it is intact. We are all born with this grace, but soon the pressures of time take over and we are forced to abandon it as an illusion. But while it lasts, yes, as long as I hold him in my arms, I will remember what was once so clear. And when time claims him and he stands on his own, then my eyes will fade along with his and we will enter the world of dreams hand in hand."

Finally they were alone again and began walking away toward the countryside. As he walked, Leo wondered what secrets the Beloved may have whispered into his ear, secrets he was sure he had missed. He hoped Francis would reveal more of his mind, declaring the lessons he was meant to discover for himself. But the silence was too profound, and Leo waited a very long time before he broke it with his words.

"We have heard so many descriptions of love this day," Leo finally said as he walked up behind his friend, "and each one has told us more about the person than the experience. I pray that you will open yourself to me now and describe what is in your heart, Francis. Talk to me of love and the passion you have discovered."

Francis kept his back toward his friend and kept on walking. It was as if a dark cloud had suddenly formed, and the weight of that cloud pushed down upon him. He listened to the wind as if it was a voice he remembered, and it spoke to him of dreams he thought he had let die. They rose above the landscape and cast long shadows that blanketed the saint. The air around him suddenly grew cold and he stood statue-like against a world only he could perceive.

"In the past, my dearest brother, you asked me to describe the fruits of love, and words flowed from my lips like milk into your mouth," Francis finally said. "Words come so easily to the one who faces away from the center, the heart which comprehends these secrets. Anyone can talk for hours about the things that appear before them as a mist, but never once touch the soul of love, that radiant source that teaches the heart about the heart. It is the one who faces inward, staring in at the rooms and dark caverns that hold thorns to wound us, who climbs to the highest branch of the highest tree and picks from that limb the sweetest fruit. Most are content to stand upon the ground and stretch toward the fruit that leans toward the earth. The rest seems unattainable—and so it is."

Leo walked over to where Francis stood and asked: "Why do you suddenly speak in this manner? A moment ago we were reveling in the passion of love, and now that very same passion has forced you inward. Speak to me of what you see now."

Tears began to form in Francis's eyes and his breath grew quick and heavy. It seemed as if he was hiding from something, a memory or a longing that slashed him like a sword. Whatever it was, he breathed it into his lungs and would not cast it away from his mind. Better to hold it like a child, he thought to himself, however heavy it may be. Better to pull it within those vast heart chambers to be loved and healed, rather than bury it again in the hidden place where only shadows live.

"I once sang the melody of love," Francis whispered, "and yet love was still so far away from me then. When I was young I would run through the streets of Assisi screaming for the beloved's scent that clung to my breast. And yet I knew nothing at all of love, save the passion that rises and falls within everyone that is foolish. Now here I am, claimed by the fire of love, laid to waste by the wind of love, consumed by the very breath of love, and yet I have nothing at all to say to you. I open my mouth to speak but my words are a muffled whisper that even I can't hear. I am mute, without a voice, without the will to look in her direction again. What will I see if I do, Brother Leo? Is her face as fair as it was when I ventured my first glance, so many years before I knew how a single moment of love can destroy one's life? Or have her features hardened, just as mine have hardened, cracked by the years that have separated us?

"Love has wrapped a gilded robe around my shoulders and has asked me to wait for her until she comes again. How long has it been? I am certain of nothing. I only know that the robe has grown heavy across my back, and I do not know how much longer I can bear its weight. There are times when I feel like flinging it into the cold river, then watch it float downstream till it has disappeared from my sight. But then I hear her voice, off somewhere in the distance, from a direction I cannot discern. It is enough to satisfy me, enough to make me wait another year perhaps. I'm cold now, and I wonder if I will never sing again."

Leo took Francis by the arm and led him over to a fallen log where they could sit. Tears were pouring from Francis' eyes as if he was suddenly seized by an invisible force that only he could see. There was nothing Leo could say to him, nothing that would help him endure this pain. He waited until Francis wiped the tears from his eyes with the sleeve of his habit.

"Please tell me," Leo pleaded. "I cannot bear to see you this way. If you are haunted by a dream that pursues you even in the day then let me enter that dream and stand by your side that we may slay this dragon together."

Francis laughed at this image. In his mind he could see Leo standing next to him holding a large stick, swinging it wildly in the direction of some fire-breathing foe. He cleared his throat and took his friend by the hand.

"My dearest Leo, I wish to confess something to you. There is weight upon my soul that I must release, otherwise I will soon be crushed. I am going to tell you something that I have never revealed to anyone, something I have never dared reveal. It has taken me years to become aware of it, though there was always a part of me that knew. We can never hide from our shadow for long, though we close our eyes and claim it is invisible to the world."

"Tell me then whatever you wish," Leo said to him. "Whatever you reveal to me, regardless of its weight, I will never speak of it to anyone."

"Oh my dearest brother, if you only knew who speaks to you now, you would become silent and would walk away from me forever. You see an image of who you want me to be, not who I truly am. I exist only in your mind, Leo. The man you see in front of you knows nothing, save the things he has heard others mention."

"How can you say these things?" Leo said to him. "Everyone in Italy loves you, and even the Pope exalts in your holiness. People come from all over Europe seeking your advice, and many of them leave behind all their worldly possessions just to follow you."

"People come to me and ask me to tell them about life, about love, and about the blessings of our Divine Lord. If they knew who I really am, if they saw the one who sits behind this facade, they would be silent, and they would look at me as they look upon anyone who knows nothing at all of love. If they knew how I have run from love and hidden my face from love's call, then they would not revere me so. They would see that I am no different from anyone they know, and they would seek the company of someone far holier than I.

"You see my brother, when I was young I had a vision of love. Love appeared before me, blinding my eyes to everything but its glory. And I lived in that place, slept in the sweet embrace of that love, and learned many of the mysteries you now seek. But then something changed. Something arose in my heart that sent me running for shelter. A sudden storm lashed against me, and I boarded up the windows of my heart to escape the pain I felt. The sound of the wind filled my ears and I cried out to God to make me deaf. But instead of silence I heard her voice, and it drove me inward, away from love's promise and into the shadow of fear."

"What is this you speak of, Francis? I feel the pain of your words, but I cannot fathom its cause. It sounds as if love has changed for you, or that you discovered a path that troubles your mind. But surely this does not mean..."

"It means exactly what I say it means. I ran from love's embrace, the possibility of a rare and wonderful love, and hid inside myself waiting for it to leave. If I had known more... if I could have sensed the sudden change of air, then perhaps I would have known what to do. But I cannot hide from who I am, and I cannot forget who she could have been to me."

"Who is it you speak of?" Leo asked. "Is there a lady who has claimed your heart that you have never mentioned to us before?"

Brother Leo meant for those words to lighten the air. It was to be a kind of joke, a way of drawing Francis out of the shadows and into the light where he could speak freely of his sorrow. Instead, there came a look in his eyes that made Leo realize his arrow had hit its true mark. Francis sat up straight upon the log and looked toward the sky. A tear fell from his eye, and it followed the contour of his face until it was absorbed into the fabric of his tattered habit.

"As I said before," Francis cried, "you do not know everything about me."

"And as I said before," Leo said as he reached out to take Francis' hand, "I am your true brother, and I will not judge you for anything you have done, or ever will do."

There was a long moment of silence between the two men, and Leo wondered if he was being presumptuous. There was nothing Francis could say or do that would change Leo's opinion of him. This was the man who saved his life. Francis was well known for his humility, but this was something more, and Leo knew it. No matter how far this well plunged into the earth's crust, Leo would never leave his brother's side. Francis seemed to feel this, as if the two men were speaking not with words, but heart to heart. He looked up at Leo and smiled. Just for a moment the sun broke through the clouds.

"It is very simple really," Francis said. "I am surprised you have not sensed it already. I am surprised that the whole world has yet to sense the truth. And what is this truth my lips avoid? Simply this: that I am in love with Clare. From the moment she came to me at the chapel of San Damiano I knew that my life would never be the same. But I also knew that ours was not an ordinary love, as if love ever could be ordinary. That is why I have run from her ever since. From the day I welcomed her into the order until the moment when you waited for us outside the chapel door, I have never once been alone with her. The current of my love is so strong that the sudden fix of her eyes would be enough to crack the dam of my indecision. When I am in her presence I have need to look away from her, in the direction of any distraction I can find. And always, as you yourself have seen, I have placed my brothers as a wall between us, blocking my view of the one whose love could rescue my life.

"And so you see, my brother, in truth I know nothing of love, but only selfishness and fear. Were it not so then love's fire would fill these empty spaces and I would claim it with strength and vigor. No, I have not claimed love. I have chosen fear as a bedmate, and loneliness as my bride."

Leo could not believe the words he heard. Was this the same man who spoke so openly about the virtues of the celibate life, whose spiritual bride he guarded as fiercely as any man would his wife? A dagger was close to his heart, and he felt the sharp chill of the blade. But then it withdrew and Leo remembered how much he loved his brother. Was he not also like any man who breathes and longs for love? And what of the heart that beats as a drum calling out for a moment of tenderness? Could it be denied, as if such desires were lower than the sacred call they had answered?

Then Leo thought of Clare, the Beloved of God, who was the first woman to understand the life Francis and the other brothers lived. She left everything just as they had done and surrendered her life to the simple lifestyle they loved. Everyone knew that there was a bond between these two saints that no one could understand, but Francis' sudden disclosure sent a wave of confusion through Leo's soul.

Then Leo squeezed his brother's hand, for the gates of his heart were suddenly flung open, just as a flower that spreads wide its petals the moment it feels the warmth of the morning sun. He wiped a tear from Francis' eye and said to him:

"It is all so clear to me now. Why are you so surprised to feel this way, to love this one who loves you so much that she gave her life in imitation of yours? You two are like mighty trees that stand at opposite sides of the garden. Their branches stretch toward the same sky and they are watered by the same storm, but to the one who stands looking, it seems obvious that these two trees are isolated and alone. And yet, look beneath the ground and one discovers a different life, for the roots are intertwined, making it impossible to say that they are separate. The roots are so vast that they support and nurture the whole garden, just as you and Clare nurture all of us."

"Would that I leave that garden and look not upon her breadth. Would that I fall..."

"No, that will not do," Leo said. "If one tree falls then the other falls as well, and the whole garden would languish. You have not broken any vow, dear Francis, nor have you disappointed us in any way. Indeed, your love inspires us all, the way you dispel hatred with your willingness to share these difficulties. Clare is your bride as sure as any man ever loved a woman, and God has called you into a holy relationship that defies the normal bounds of custom. This is not something to decry, but to follow with great joy. Our Lord has bestowed upon you a precious gift, and it is right that you accept this prize with gratitude and still more love."

Francis looked into Leo's eyes for a long moment, and it seemed as if the cloud of despair had vanished at last. "You have inhaled today's prayer into your lungs and now exhale it into my mouth," he said. "You are more than a worthy companion, Leo, you are a true friend. And your prayer has been answered, just as mine is fulfilled through your words. You may continue with me as far as you choose, all the way to the feet of the Sultan if that is your desire. How can I send you back now? What if I need your counsel again? No, you will be at my side from this moment on."

ver the next several days, Francis and Leo passed through many villages, and whenever they saw a chapel or a monastery they would stop and pray to show reverence. Leo preferred to kneel in the back praying quietly by himself. Francis, on the other hand, would walk to the front of each church, stand in the center of the altar, then fall and prostrate himself before the Sacred Sacrament, remaining in that motionless position for at least half an hour. He would then stand and begin singing at full voice, making up the words as he went along. In this way, he would praise the Divine, and though Leo could not bring himself to join Francis in this display, it filled him with great joy to witness the amazing devotion exhibited by his brother.

One day when they were engaged in prayer, a monk burst into the chapel and disrupted them both. He was short and round, and as he barreled up the aisle, Leo could see his eyes bulging with anger. He stopped at the altar, genuflected, then launched himself at Francis. Francis, however, did not resist the assault. The monk grabbed hold of his habit and dragged his down the aisle, then out the door. Leo ran behind them overcome with fear.

"What is the meaning of this outrage," the monk screamed. "How dare you desecrate our chapel in this way? You are nothing more than indigent beggars and have no right entering such a holy place. What were you thinking?"

Francis looked at the angry man with the eyes of a child and didn't say a word. The monk, however, continued to huff and puff deeply and held his body as if ready to do battle. "Go on," the monk screamed, "answer me, man. What were you doing in there?"

But the two brothers remained silent, and Francis continued to look deep into the monk's eyes with love and compassion. Seconds later the man relaxed his stance and softened his expression. Leo watched this transformation with utter amazement. He was sure the monk was about to beat them but instead he became very quiet and sat down on the step of the chapel.

"Perhaps I have overreacted," the monk said. "Please, for the love of God, forgive me. I am responsible for maintaining this and several other chapels in this area and there have been many vagrants to chase away. But I sense no ill intent from you. Who are you and why are you here?"

"We are peace pilgrims on our way to the Crusades," Francis said. "I intend to preach the gospel to the Muslims and convert the Sultan. In this way we will end the war and bring peace to our land."

The month nearly fell backwards as he laughed. "You are not vagrants, you are mad," he said to them. "You cannot preach toe the Muslims. They are heathens and deserve the vengeance of Christ. You will surely be killed if you go anywhere near the Crusades. I suggest you return to wherever you came from and leave these matters to Holy Mother Church."

Francis stood over the man and continued looking at him with loving, childlike eyes. The monk was suddenly overcome with a feeling he did not understand, and stood to face the two men. His eyes began to fill with tears, and he reached out and placed his hand on Francis' arm.

"Or I may be wrong. Once again, I am sorry for the manner in which I treated you. May the good Lord be with you on your journey."

The monk turned and walked away, obviously overwhelmed by the encounter. He went off to find a quiet place to reflect on the strange way he had reacted to the unusual little man he evicted from the chapel.

Leo turned toward Francis with confused eyes, for he was as stupefied as the monk had been. He didn't say a word, but Francis knew what he was thinking.

"Why are you so confused by what you have seen?" Francis asked him. "When we allow ourselves to be used as instruments of peace, miracles occur naturally. We become channels of Divine Light when we step back and surrender to the Will of God. No illusion can withstand the tide of light, and the hardened heart is instantly softened."

"You hardly said a word to that man, and yet he was completely transformed by you. I am sure that this is my next lesson in peace."

Francis motioned for Leo to follow him and they continued their journey. Once they were back on the road, Francis continued.

"There is a language which the heart understands but the ear cannot hear," he said. "Each one of us knows that language and instantly responds to it. It is not spoken with the mouth or with words, but with the eyes and the spirit. It is like a song that slides close to the heart when we are not aware and moves us in a way we cannot understand. The effect is immediate, stronger than wine or the most potent medicine we know. We need only sense the approach of this song and we are washed clean of discord, levelled by the delicate scent of its sweet bloom."

"Tell me then, what is this thing that so transformed the monk, and which has the power to transmute the energies of hatred and fear?"

"It is love, Brother Leo, only love. There is no more powerful force in all the universe than a heart centered in this holy state. The anger of our brother monk could not withstand the energy of it. The hatred he felt was not toward us at all, but from a deeper longing he was unaware of. By offering love where an attack seemed to exist, God healed that empty place and smoothed it in a manner that escaped his mind, but not his heart. Everything we ever do is either a gift of love or a call for love. Therefore, the only proper response in either situation is love. Then we become like the wind that cools everyone who stands in the open field, regardless of how worthy we judge that one to be."

"How do we offer this gift to another?" Brother Leo asked.

"That is a very good question, my brother. There is a way of looking into the eyes of another that opens the door of the heart, becoming a fountain from which another can drink. There is a simple exercise I will teach you that will help you see in this way. When you have learned this exercise and have practiced it for a while, you will not think the transformation of our brother monk strange at all.

"When we look at another we have a choice which we are not normally conscious of. Most of us look into the eyes of a person and focus on the ways they seem different from us. They look different, they act different, and they have a past that is very different from our own. It is the ego that perceives these things, not the spirit. The ego has forgotten that there is an underlying unity that binds us together, making of us one being, one extension of the Holy Mind of God. It would rather focus on the ways we are special and distinct rather than see the truth that the spirit perceives.

"The foundation of these two ways of 'seeing' is different as well. The 'self' which the ego perceives springs from a feeling of separation and disconnectedness. Therefore, its foundation is fear and it is always focused on protecting the ways in which it is different from others. The foundation of the spirit's vision is quite different—it is love, and it seeks to join rather than separate. When we look at another through the eyes of the ego, we reinforce the part of the other that wants to be separate and alone. But when we look through the eyes of spirit, seeing past all the illusions that seem to separate us, we reinforce the part of the other that longs for love. They feel our gift at an intuitive level, beyond the intellect. They may not even know what is happening, but they feel a sense of freedom in your gaze that fills them and reminds them of their truest nature."

"But how do I practice this art, Brother Francis?" Leo asked.

"I will tell you how," he said. "When you stand in front of another, pretend that they are wearing a mask. The fact is, as long as you are judging the outer appearance of another, you are seeing only their mask, or the ways they hide from the truth within them. Now imagine that you are looking through the slits in that mask, past the charade to the 'real' face. This is the identity behind the mask, what we will call the 'true' self. Focus on that face rather than the one the mask portrays. See the truth in that person, the soul that is one with the Divine. You are one with that soul as well, for it is but another aspect of your own perfection. If you look at this person in such a way then the wall of separation begin to fade and you see them in the same manner as God. And isn't this the true goal of our spiritual life, to see God as God sees, and to love as God loves?"

"And what will happen then?"

"You have seen for yourself what will happen. The other person realizes what you have done, not consciously but at a deeper, more essential level. They sense that you are loving them for who they are, not what they are not. And they will respond to that love, though they may not realize what it is that they are doing. Each person you meet longs to be seen through the eyes of truth, and that is what we are called to do, Brother Leo. Our monk friend felt the gaze of the Divine upon his soul, the sense that he was being seen for who he really is. And when he did, he was no longer able to attack us. He laid down his sword and accepted the gift he was offered. When we do this to everyone we meet, then we become instruments of transformation, which is the act of becoming co-conspirators with God."

Then Francis stopped in the middle of the road and fell to his knees. He was suddenly overcome with the love of God and cried out in a loud voice, "Let us repeat the prayer we have focused on these past few days. Brother Leo. 'Lord, where there is hatred, let me bring love.' Help me become the extension of your holy vision, that I may look upon your creation with the eyes of love. Teach me what it means to perceive the truth wherever I go, and to be a witness to your Divine plan. Stir the center of my being that I may see as you see and love as you love. Then I will truly know who you are, my Beloved, simply because I have seen you within everyone and everything."

Chapter Five

"Where there is injury, pardon"

eo asked Francis, "You never answered my question, what will you say to the Sultan when you finally arrive in the land of the Muslims?"

Francis stopped along the side of the road and thought for a moment. "I do not know what I will say," he finally admitted. "Let's hope I don't say a word."

"What do you mean? Surely you will not stand in front of him in silence. You are not intending to..."

"What I mean, Brother Leo, is that I have nothing to say, but I pray the Lord will say a great deal through me. That is what the prayer, 'Make me an instrument of your peace' means. I am but the mouth piece of the Divine. As I release my judgments, then God can use me in ways I could not imagine before. If I act on my own, then I act from a place of weakness, not in union with the eternal strength that could be mine. It is mine but to surrender and step back into the arms of the Beloved, not step forward and think that I have the answer. I assure you, Brother Leo, we would all be in a great deal of trouble if I thought I knew anything at all."

"But what if you are brought before the Sultan and God has nothing to say?" Leo asked, desperately trying to grasp Francis' words. "How do you know when you are being used as an instrument?"

"It is God's Will that we be used as instruments of peace every moment of our lives, my dearest Leo. This brings us to the second stage of spiritual growth—trust. Once we have stepped back and surrendered to the Divine, we must then learn to trust the new vision of reality we are shown. It is the greatest joy of God to show us the secrets of the Kingdom, but only when we are able to surrender the world we think we made and trust reality itself. Only then will our half-closed eyes perceive the light that illumines the 'real world'. This is the world that has been reserved for us since the beginning of time, the Peaceful Kingdom that was saved from the unholy sight of sin and death, the eternal home we never left, except in our imagination."

"But how do we accept this vision?" Leo asked. "Please forgive my pace, but your words are so high. It is difficult for me to climb this steep ladder and breathe the thin air which you swim in. You must give me some practical exercise, some way to integrate those holy words in my life."

"Then let this be your prayer today: 'Lord, where there is

injury, pardon.' This simple line has everything you will need. This holy prayer illustrates the single most important tool we have in this process of transformation: forgiveness. It is the act of attuning our minds to the mind of God, thinking like God, seeing as God sees. Forgiveness is the closest we can come to the gates of Heaven, and still find ourselves in the world. Through this blessed practice, your mind will ascend to perception's highest peak where no secret is hidden from you, and no truth remains unattained."

"Are you saying that in order to think and see as God we must learn to forgive those who have done some wrong to us?"

"I am saying that if you want to think and see as God, you must understand that the wrong you think was committed against you never occurred at all."

"But I don't understand," Leo gasped. "How can I see something, then not see it?"

"There was once a man who fell into a deep sleep," Francis said to him. "While he was asleep, he dreamed that his neighbor committed some terrible sin against him. He was so enraged that he brought his neighbor to trial and saw that he was convicted of the crime. But just before his neighbor was hauled off to jail, the man woke up and found that it was all just a dream.

"'This will not do,' he said to himself. 'I will not allow my neighbor to get away with this crime just because I am no longer asleep and dreaming.' He therefore rose from his bed, put on his clothes and walked to his neighbor's house. The neighbor, unaware of the dream, thought his friend had come for morning coffee, but instead he was dragged from his house and beaten in his own yard. He lay there, half-conscious, wondering what he had done to deserve this punishment. His neighbor said to him, 'Now you will think twice before stealing my belongings.' The man who was beaten sat up and said, 'I don't know what you are talking about, for I have not stolen a thing from you.' But the first man went back to his home, satisfied he had repaid the man for the crime."

"But the man was insane," Leo said. "He was not able to tell the difference between what he had dreamed and what actually happened."

"And this is the true meaning of forgiveness, Brother Leo. When you are able to tell the difference between your dream world and reality itself, you will no longer make another person guilty of a crime you believe they committed. It is our task to focus on innocence, not guilt. Stay with the prayer I have given you today. 'Lord, where there is injury, pardon.' Then you will enter into the Mind of God, and begin to think as God thinks, and see as God sees.

hey heard the story long before they had reached the village of Gubbio. A fierce wolf, which was said to live near the town, had already killed several small children (or so the passer-by claimed). It had struck fear in the hearts of everyone in the village, and they were determined to kill this creature, lest they themselves be killed.

"Come, we are going to Gubbio to see about this wolf," Francis told Leo.

"But Francis, Gubbio is at least a day in the wrong direction. Couldn't we…"

"Even if it were three days out of the way, or a week… still we must go." Francis stopped and looked at Leo with deep, compassionate eyes. "This wolf is my brother, just as you are my brother. I can feel its pain, and the deep wound that has been cut into its soul. Imagine how it would feel to be despised by a whole town, to be mocked and marked for death. And what if it were all a misunderstanding? What if this creature has been injured in some way and has forgotten how to respond in love? Yes, Leo, we are going to make peace between the wolf and the people of Gubbio. Then we will learn for ourselves what it means to forgive."

"How is forgiveness required in bringing an end to this dispute?" Leo asked.

"That is what you must discover for yourself, my brother. Remember your prayer today: 'Where there is injury, pardon.' This creature is more kin to us than you know, Leo. I see my own reflection in the fierceness of his eyes."

Leo understood exactly what Francis meant. He was like the 'Wolf of Assisi,' especially during those lonely years when he was cast from the city and despised even by his family. Francis had surely felt the isolation this wolf now felt, so it was no surprise that he would divert their plans to answer its plea for help.

When they arrived in Gubbio, Francis headed straight for the town's main square and braced himself atop a large stone fountain. People began to gather around him, and he spoke to them about the love God possesses for all creatures.

"People of Gubbio, I come to you now as one who has heard the voice of God in the creatures and the birds you see all around you, yea, even in the fields around your village. Sometimes when I am near my own home, I love to lie upon the ground with one ear pressed against the ground, and I listen to the gentle whispering of the earth. She says things to me that I can hardly believe, and my soul rejoices when I hear them. She tells me that we are all holy in the eyes of our Divine Parent, including the creatures of the earth that fill God's heart with an ever expanding joy. Even these creatures which you fear are loved by God, for each one of them holds a place in the Heavenly Kingdom."

"All except the wolf that eats our children," a large man screamed at the top of his lungs. "Such a creature is despised in the eyes of God."

"Show me this wolf that I may converse with it, reminding it of God's mercy," Francis said to the man. "Perhaps then this creature you fear will repent, just as we are all asked to repent, and enter once again into your favor."

The man began to laugh out loud and scoffed at the saint. "We know who you are," he said. "You are that lunatic from Assisi, the one who talks to the animals and birds. I would love to see you converse with this our enemy. It will be the end of you if you try."

Then a small round woman pushed her way through the crowd. "These men are cowards," she said to Francis. "I will take you to the wolf's lair, and I will stand at your side when you confront the creature. I am not afraid of the wolf, nor of these pathetic animals in this village who call themselves men."

A roar rose from the crowd and a minute later they were all marching to the countryside behind Francis, and the woman strutted along as if she were a queen. After some time they came to a cliff and the crowd would not go farther. Francis could see the cave they pointed to, and with the woman still at his side he headed straight toward its mouth.

While all of this was happening, Leo stood back from the crowd and sketched everything he saw. His hands flashed across the pad and he did his best to capture Francis as he had clung to the top of the fountain, or as he confidently marched off with the woman. And yet a part of him was afraid that the crowd might be right. What if this was the end of his companion? He didn't dare consider this terrible thought even for a second longer.

When Francis and the woman were halfway to the cave, they heard the sound of pounding feet and grinding teeth behind them. They spun around and saw the enormous wolf, its fangs bared and its muscles taut, racing toward them. The woman fell to the ground in fear, and Francis could hear the great gasp that rose from the crowd a short distance away. But this would not be the moment of his death. He folded his hands in front of him and began slowly walking in the direction of the charging wolf, which was clearly confused by this advance. Then the animal stopped no more than twenty feet away from Francis and began pacing to and fro.

The wolf growled a deep growl and tried to frighten Francis with the fierce sound. Francis, unmoved by this display, sat down upon the ground and took out a small wooden flute. As Francis played the flute, the wolf began to slow its pacing back and forth until it finally sat down a little distance in front of the strange little man.

No one in the crowd could hear what Francis said to the wolf, but he spoke for a very long time, his hands moving about as they would during any conversation, and the wolf seemed to actually be listening to him. After some time the wolf stood up and walked over to Francis until it stood directly in front of him. Then it sat down again and held out its paw, and the two creatures of God shook to seal whatever deal they had made. Francis then stood up, walked back to the woman who was now watching the whole scene, then took her by the arm and led her back to the crowd. The wolf never moved, but sat watching them with hopeful eyes.

"People of Gubbio," Francis said to the crowd, "may I present to you the new guardian of your village. This wolf you see has agreed to protect all of you, granted, of course, that you forgive him his previous deeds and lay aside any desire to do him harm. If you agree, this wolf will watch over your village by night so that no evil thing may come to you."

The people could not believe their ears. Had Francis actually struck a deal with this creature that the bravest among them were afraid to go near? They looked across the field and saw the wolf watching them, as if waiting for the deal to be accepted.

"Of course," the round woman said as she waved her fist in the air, "let anyone even think of harming that wolf and they will have to deal with me. Then they will know how it feels to have someone's teeth upon their neck."

The crowd roared again and the deal was sealed.

Later that night as Francis and Leo walked along the lonely road together, Leo had to find out what happened when Francis was alone with the wolf.

"It is very simple," Francis said. "I looked upon my brother just as God looks upon him."

"What do you mean?" Leo asked.

"This, my dear brother, is the essence of everything I have to teach to you. Ours is not to look upon each other and see what is different, sinful, and base. It is our calling to 'See as God sees,' which is through the eyes of holiness itself. And it is the same with the creatures of God. We are asked to perceive all God's creatures with love and grace, no matter how they appear or act. This wolf you saw was as afraid as the citizens of Gubbio. Imagine how you would feel if an entire population ran from you, threw stones at you, and assailed you in many different ways. Your heart would grow cold and you would forget the love that gave you to the earth and sky."

"But I saw you speaking to the wolf," Leo said to him. "It was almost as if the wolf understood your words. What could you say..."

"My words were nothing," Francis said. "It was my heart that spoke to the wolf, and the wolf understood me. I saw the fierce creature through the eyes of compassion, that is all. Compassion always gives rise to forgiveness, and forgiveness always leads to love. These things are inseparable in the eyes of our Blessed Lord. And so they are inseparable in our eyes as well. When we see all of God's creatures in this light, then we will realize that there is no sin that cannot be forgiven, no offense that cannot be pardoned, and no deed that cannot be bent toward truth. Indeed, when we see through the eyes of God, then we realize that we are already forgiven, and it is there, Brother Leo, that you must look to find the real meaning of today's prayer."

Chapter Six

"Where there is doubt, bring your faith"

eo was beginning to believe that he would never capture the essence of the saint he loved upon his pad. He had not noticed how many faces his brother could show, for each day a new man would rise demanding a new page upon which a whole new life would appear. And each one of these faces required new attention, just as the sun rises in the East morning after morning but never once casts the same shadow upon the same ground.

He began to wonder if he was up to the sacred task to which he was bound through holy obedience. It was not the pen that had failed him, nor was it the coarse paper upon which he would often draw. It was his mind and perhaps even his spirit that rose in defiance. Leo even began to wonder if he was worthy to travel at Francis' side on this journey of peace. These demons raged a war within his soul and cast a spell of doubt over his hand. He sat down with his back against a large rock and wondered if he should return to Assisi alone.

It was very early in the morning and Francis was off wandering the countryside in prayer when Leo underwent this trial. Francis sensed the sudden change of air even though he was still a good distance away from his friend, and he hastened to return. When he arrived at the spot where they had spent the night, he saw Leo crouched in a small ball with his drawing pad flung against a pile of stones. Leo did not even raise his head when he heard Francis approach, but turned away from him in shame.

"Why do you turn away from me?" Francis asked. "Have I proven such a poor companion that you would now choose this rock as your friend and this damp ground as your confessor?"

Leo lifted his head and looked into Francis' eyes. They were like radiant pools of light that filled the dark spaces of his torment, melting the shadows that moments earlier had embraced him. He wanted to reach out and touch Francis' hand, and he started to, but then the demon grabbed hold of him again and he shrunk back against the boulder.

"Go away and leave me here," Leo told him as he turned away. "I am not worthy to walk at your side, let alone fulfill the commission that was given to me. Each time I look within to find the muse that would inspire my hand, it shrinks into the empty caves where I hide in fear. And there it stays, for I am not worthy to look upon such a holy face as yours, let alone sketch a portrait that will be loved by so many generations."

Francis fell back against the rock as if he was suddenly struck by a great blow, then raised both hands to his face and began to weep. Leo was so surprised by this that he sat up straight and wrapped his arms around the saint. The doubt that had claimed him was gone and he became instead a blanket that would protect Francis from the cold wind that had so quickly lashed against him.

"You are right to leave me, Leo. For I am a poor sinner who is not worthy of the company of one as true as you. I beg that you leave me here and go on to Syria alone. Tell everyone that you are the 'Saint of Assisi,' the man who has aroused such great fervor, causing men and women to cast away their wealth and serve God in joy. It would be far more true to say these things about you, my brother, than about the wretched soul who sits beside you now."

Leo was shaken by these words. Was this not the same man who inspired his life, his path, yes, even his soul? Indeed, half of Europe praised his name and called him the 'Troubadour of God,' or the 'Flute of Holiness.' How could Francis cower in such a manner, throwing himself before God as a common sinner? Leo was simple, yes, more simple than most, but he understood the sense of great crime and undue weight that had fallen across his brother's back.

"How can you say these things?" Leo whispered into Francis' ear. "You are my guide... my light. You are anything but a sinner."

Francis pulled away and wiped the tears from his eyes. "You do not understand," he said. "I am nothing without the grace of God. Just as you doubt the talent bestowed upon your hand by our Divine Parent, so do I sometimes doubt my station. You look at me and see an image you create in your mind, while I look to that deeper well, that dark cavern where the long dead shadows of my youth still live. Sometimes I throw the bucket of my awareness down that dark hole and I pull from the well the illusions of my past. And then I lay them before God as a sacrifice upon the altar of love to be purified and undone. I am each one of these faces, not just the one that cries to you now. I am equally humbled by the shadow of my past and the illumination of my purified soul."

"It is I who am humbled to wait upon such a servant of God," Leo said as he turned his face away. "Who am I to walk beside you, or to sketch your blessed countenance? My hand shakes when I think about it, let alone when I lay the pencil to the pad. I look at your lips but do not see flesh at all. Instead I see you as you kiss the wounds of a leper, or I hear the song of freedom that you often sing. I look to draw your hands, but they dissolve into the hands of all those you have touched and healed. How am I to draw this vapor of grace that changes each time I look upon it?"

"As I said before, dear brother, these things are in your mind, as is the doubt you feel. The mind has two directions in which it can turn—one direction being toward the Light and the other away from it. The Light itself will inspire a whole succession of images, depending, of course, upon your willingness to behold its radiance. Turn your face into its blessed warmth and your mind is filled with faith. Turn away and the doubt you feel rushes in like a flood. Which do you desire? Will you turn and face the grace that is yours, or choose instead the shadow you cast upon the ground?"

"I do not understand, Francis. How can I release this doubt, even if it is a mental decision I make? It seems to have saturated my life, filling every empty crevice I behold."

By now Francis' heart was on fire, and the anguish he felt had disappeared. He stood up and mounted the rock that served as their back-rest, then opened his arms so that the wind would blow against his whole body.

"You can't," Francis screamed. "You can do nothing, save what is done through you when you surrender to the grace of God. This doubt you feel is like a chain you have locked to your own ankles. The key is gone and you have no way of releasing yourself from this bondage. But the Holy Spirit has not forgotten how and holds the key you have lost. It waits upon your consent, ready at any moment to leap into service. But it too is tied until the moment you ask for help. Only then can it give to you the freedom that is yours."

"Tell me how to ask," Leo implored. "I do not want the weight of this doubt anymore. I am willing to do whatever you say."

Francis jumped from the boulder and landed in front of Brother Leo. Then he put his hands on Leo's shoulders and looked deep into his eyes.

"Do you really mean that what you say?" he asked. "Are you willing to lay aside every limiting belief that has imprisoned your creative soul? Are you ready to surrender everything, especially your doubts, then trust what the spirit of truth reveals?"

"I am ready," Leo said to him.

Francis released his grip on Leo and stepped away from him. "Then it is done," he said. "That is all God requires of you."

"But how can it be so easy?" Leo asked with confused eyes. "Surely more is required of me."

"Why? Isn't your surrender enough? Isn't your willingness to trust enough? Let me tell you a little secret, my dear brother. If you can accept what I'm about to tell you, then the rest will be easy. Ready? Your surrender and trust are enough for God; now you have to let them be enough for you."

"What do you mean?"

"Just what I said to you. Oh, if only we would allow the simplicity of God's love to be enough. Your '**yes**' is enough for God. Do you understand? You said you were willing to surrender and trust God; now you have to be willing to let it be enough. You can make it more complicated if you want, but your need to do so will just be another chain that binds you.

"This is what Christ meant when he asked us to live like the birds of the air. They keep nothing for themselves, they gather nothing in barns nor store their water in vast containers. Yet God watches over them, provides for them, and gives them everything they need to soar. We, in our arrogance, have more faith in ourselves than in the pulse of life itself. We cut ourselves from the Divine River of Holiness and gather our possessions around us in fear. We fool ourselves into believing that the more riches we have, the more secure and happy we will be. The opposite is true. The result of any fearful thought system is always more fear. How can lack and fear lead to abundance and love?

"When we live in faith we cling to nothing, save our longing for the Divine. God is our infinite supply, and when we tap that source we are never denied full satisfaction. Do you remember our Beloved Lord speaking in the gospel of a woman who gave her last copper coin for the love of God? He invites us to live just like her, offering our lives to the Divine without demand or misgiving, confident that we will receive a hundred times more in the Kingdom of God."

Then Francis stopped and looked deep into Leo's eyes. "Let this be your prayer today: 'Lord, where there is doubt, bring your faith.' Do you see how simple praying can be, my brother? The world offers one choice and God answers with another. Which will you choose—lack or infinite supply, doubt or faith? When you have made the choice given to you by God, you will be ready to take the next step, the experience that lies past faith, the deeper reality which is our destiny.

"God is willing to replace your illusions with the truth, or in other words, take your doubt and give you faith instead. And yet this gift which has been freely given must now be freely received. You will never be forced to accept truth, but it will be offered to you in so many ways.

"You are afraid you cannot draw a picture of me that will be sufficient, and you doubt the talent that has been showered upon you by the Beloved. I'm going to tell you something now that may shock you, but this truth, if you breathe it into your lungs, can also set you free. 'You cannot draw a portrait of me or anyone that is sufficient.' It is impossible. Are you surprised? And yet here is more—if you learn to surrender and trust, then a portrait will be drawn 'through' you that has the power to transform the whole world. Do you understand the difference?

"You can never fulfill the destiny given to you by God on your own. And yet, when you surrender to the living spring that flows through every atom of your being every moment of every day, then everything you do, everything you touch, fulfills your destiny. Alone you can do nothing, my brother, but when aligned with the Heart and Mind of God, all things are done through you."

"I will surrender and give my trust and in this way I will receive the faith you described." Leo said. "But what is that thing that lies past faith, Brother Francis? Tell me about this reality which is our destiny."

"It is certainty," Francis said to him. It is the certainty that we are children of the Divine, and that we will always be looked after. It begins with faith, which is of the mind, but through practice we come to a deeper experience where we simply know what is true. Certainty is the product of a heart bent on love alone. This is where your prayer will lead you, Brother Leo. And when you come to this place, you will be near the gates of Heaven, so close that you will smell the sweetness of the Garden of the Divine.

"It is a gift that even the Angels envy, and I say to you that it is the ultimate goal that you can hope to attain. Once you have stepped away from doubt and received the faith I have described, then you are a single step away from the true goal— **certainty**. When you have felt the rapture of this tide, then even faith will seem to you a trivial thing. When you are **certain** of God's love for you, then everything else takes its place behind your enlightenment."

Chapter Seven

"Where there is despair, hope"

he next day Francis and Leo found themselves walking through a region that was known for its vineyards and rich grapes. And though it was nearly the season when men gather the ripened fruit and press it into wine, they did not see any activity at all. They had, in fact, walked for many miles without seeing a single person, and they began to wonder what this meant.

"Perhaps this is a day of rest," Leo said. "Or is it a holiday that we have forgotten and the workers are gathered together in some church or in their homes eating or asleep?"

"No, it is not a day of rest, my brother, and neither have we forgotten a holy feast. An area such as this follows the seasons as they would a clock, and when the time of harvest arrives they do not tarry in their homes or rest with their families. Look at the withered vines and the malnourished grapes. Some famine has befallen this region, and the crop seems lost."

Just then they looked ahead and saw a man standing in the field bent over the vine as if examining the grapes. His face was red from the hot sun and his expression was like steel. Francis ran until he stood very near the man, then he raised his voice saying:

"Dear brother, can you tell us what has happened here?"

The man stood up and walked over to the saint, arriving about the same time as Leo. He held in his hand a few leaves and five or six dried grapes. Anyone could see what had happened.

"You must be a traveler to ask such a question," he said. "Look at the earth and you will know what this means. It has not rained in nearly two months. The grapes are near dead and our very lives are now at risk. My family owns nearly everything you see here and we are accustomed to providing jobs and food for more than I dare say. Yet now I barely have enough money to last till next season's crop, so it will be impossible to help the others."

Francis was moved with compassion for he could tell that this was a good and honorable man. He stepped forward until they stood only a few feet apart.

"Would that your compassion were rain and your honor like clouds, this whole valley would be as a flood. I can feel your despair, my friend, for your family and all those you love."

"You are friars, are you not?" the man said. "I have heard stories of your founder, the one they call the 'Saint of Assisi.' Perhaps if he came here to pray, then God would hear our call. Can you call to him and convey this our desperate plea?"

Leo looked over at his companion and wondered what he would say. Francis gave no indication at all that he was the man the farmer spoke of. He instead curled his lips and acted as if he despised this one.

"Yes, I know the one you speak of," Francis said. "He is the son of Pietro Bernadone, a rich man's son, and I fear he has never truly lost his taste for the fine garments he once wore."

"But I am told he is a humble man, the greatest in Italy. Men and women all over Europe have left fields and homes to follow his example."

"I can only speak of what I have seen," Francis said as he turned away. "It is true that many people proclaim his grace, but I strive to see the greater picture, the truth that lies past this man's life."

"What do you mean?" Leo asked, as if he was anxious to enter this game.

"Well, this man you speak of, the one you say is a saint... I have known him for many years. I too was moved by his ideals, but my experience has shown me that he is just a man, no different from either of you. His one saving grace is that he seeks for himself the highest order, that of imitating our Blessed Lord. So why would you imitate the imitator? Choose instead the heart of Christ, and cling to that heart as you would your breath. Then your lungs will be filled with the Light of all Lights, and that radiance will illuminate every aspect of your life."

"Yes… I understand these words," the farmer said. "But still, if you know this man as you say, I beg you to invite him here. Let him choose to come or to ignore my plea, then we will hope for our luck to change."

Francis walked back over to where the man stood and placed his hand on his shoulder. "Invite us to your home," he said. "Give us the pleasure of a few sips of wine, then I promise I will see what I can do."

The farmer led Francis and Leo to his house and bid them welcome. It was a modest home, though clean and tasteful, nothing at all like the house where Francis was raised. His father liked to collect the elaborate ornaments he'd bought from nomadic caravans, the same caravans that sold him the fine silk that filled his shop in the center of Assisi. When he was young Francis loved to wrap himself in the long stretches of cloth, holding the smooth fabric against his naked skin. So much had changed since those days, he thought to himself. Now he preferred the rough habit he had sewn together from discarded pieces of cloth over the rarest silk shirt.

"Lucia, come and meet our guests," the man yelled as he opened the door that led to the kitchen. A beautiful dark haired woman with ivory skin came through the door drying her hands with a towel, and when her eyes met Francis she dropped the towel on the floor and stared in disbelief.

"Lucia, these men know the 'Saint of Assisi,' the one you speak of so often. They are his brothers and have agreed to invite him to our region and home. Maybe this drought is a curse and the presence of this one could persuade God to lift its weight and bless us with rain. There is still time, if only the clouds would fill with tears and have compassion on us, then the grapes would be saved and we would survive this dry season."

Francis smiled at Lucia, for he knew she was on to him. Leo too could sense her confusion, and he wondered what she would do. After all, Francis was well known throughout Italy and thousands had heard him preach. If this woman spoke often of the saint, as her husband said, then perhaps she had seen him and heard his words.

"Welcome to our home, brothers," Lucia said, regaining her composure. "My husband is correct in what he says. I speak often of your Brother Francis, for I am profoundly moved by the life he leads, and the manner in which he serves God. Were it not for this demanding fool and the children I have borne him, I would be with sister Clare even now singing the praise of voluntary simplicity."

"There are many paths to God," Francis told her, "and the one you have chosen is no less than our vocation. Blessed poverty, or simplicity, begins in the heart and extends into the world. It is the heart, then, that God perceives, and the fruit that falls from that tree will feed many."

"Would that fruit would fall from the vine," the farmer said. "This is my prayer. And if it must rise like smoke to heaven, carried upon the wings of this man from Assisi, then so be it."

By the time the man had finished saying these words, Lucia had already set the table with cheese and bread. Then the farmer walked over to the cupboard and after opening the door pulled out a bottle of his finest wine.

"Please, brothers, sit for awhile and I will pour you a glass of last season's finest blend. Then you will understand what the world is missing if our production falls."

As they walked in the direction of the table, Francis took Leo by the arm and whispered into his ear: "I want to give you your prayer for the day, Leo. It is: 'Lord, where there is despair, bring your hope.' We are bound to see this prayer fulfilled in our midst."

The farmer poured the wine with great care and pride, for it was true that his was the most famous vineyard in the entire region. Francis lifted the glass then took a piece of bread from the plate, and looking toward Heaven said:

"Beloved One, when our Master and Lord walked among us, he asked us to take the simple things of life and use them to remember him. It was during his last meal with his friends that he took what was on the table, ordinary things since this was the Passover meal, bread and wine, and he gave thanks. And though hours later his friends were stricken with despair because their Master had died, they learned the true meaning of hope when three days later he walked among them again. They did not forget the one that gave them life and so their hope was fulfilled. And so we remember him now, the one who gives us life, who showed us how to see the Divine in the ordinary gifts of life.

"And now we take these same ordinary things, bread and wine, and we remember the way Jesus loved us. He told us to desire one thing and one thing alone—the Kingdom of God. And if we fix our gaze upon this Heavenly goal then everything else will be given to us as well. We feel this reality as we share this meal, these gifts, and we give all our cares to the one who answers all our prayers. We will not name them, Beloved One, for you already know what we need. We put our hope in you, and in your mercy, and we cast our despair to the fire of your love to be cleansed."

Then Francis passed the glass of wine to the others, and he gave them each a piece of bread. Lucia wept openly at the table, and her husband buried his head in his hands so as not to show his tears.

Francis and Leo had no way of knowing what happened next. They left the house after they finished their meal and were soon on their way toward the sea. A day later clouds began to form over the valley and a powerful rain fell over that whole region of Italy. For days the ground sang for joy as more rain fell, and two weeks later the grapes revived and produced the best wine in over a decade.

Chapter Eight

"Where there is darkness, bring your light"

s they approached the sea, Francis said to Leo, "There is a fire burning in my soul that no worldly pleasure can extinguish. Even if all these waves washed over my life, still would I burn with this Holy Desire. It is a sacred fire I speak of, Leo, a flame that requires no wood to burn, no oil or even coal to live. Its fuel is love, a deep incomprehensible love that radiates out and illumines the whole world. This is the reason we cross the sea to stand before the Sultan and sing this song of peace. I wish to burn him alive in the love I feel. Yes, did you hear what I said—

'burn him alive.' Earthly fire kills and destroys, while the fire we seek brings eternal life to what was cold and dead."

They had come to a small coastal town that had boats to carry travelers across the Adriatic. It was renowned for being the port where thousands of soldiers left their homeland to fight in the Great War. This seemed to fill Francis with an even greater joy, for the idea of sailing with Crusaders on their way to battle fit into his plans wonderfully.

"Think what this means," he said to Brother Leo. "These men were told that it is noble and just to kill in the name of Christ, and they have believed it. Why else would they leave everything and risk their very lives to defend Holy Mother Church? How easily we forget the words of our Blessed Lord who said, 'Love your enemy, do good to those who hate you, bless those who curse you and pray for those who abuse you.' Was this not the same man who told us not to resist evil, and that if a person strikes us on one cheek we should turn and offer the other? Why have we cast this holy lesson aside and decided that there are times to listen to Jesus, and times not to?

"Do you realize that if we sail with these men we could plant the seed that would end this war? Our job, my brother, is to teach the truth to everyone, and when everything else fails, to actually use words. Our presence alone could be enough to instill within these brave men the truth our Lord taught. Imagine if they discovered that truth and decided to march upon the Muslims in peace. They would lay their weapons on the ground and walk toward their brother soldiers with their arms open in joy. And imagine what the Muslims will think about this. They will turn toward one another and say, 'This is not at all what we expected. Maybe Allah wants us to embrace one another and lay aside our grievances.'

"Then the Christians and the Muslims would start a little community, much as we have done, and word would soon get out that the war had come to an end, if only in that one place. Men and women would then come to that place to see what had happened, and that community would grow and grow until it is larger than both Islam and Christendom combined. Imagine what that would be like, Brother Leo, all because we chose to book passage on a boat in this town."

Francis and Leo walked to the dock and saw that there was a large boat preparing to leave that day. As they suspected it was hired to carry nearly one hundred men to war, and Francis immediately went to find the boat's captain.

"Honorable captain," Francis said to the man once he was found. "We are on an errand from our Blessed Lord who desires an end to this war and who chooses peace for us all. But we are poor men, having cast aside all our earthly possessions in the service of God. We pray that you will give us safe passage to the other side of this great sea that we may fulfill our charge. I promise that this deed will not go unseen by God when the Peaceful Kingdom is established on earth."

But the captain of the boat was not a spiritual man and desired instead the income he could receive, growing rich from battle and death. He therefore hired Francis and Leo to serve the soldiers on the trip, bringing them food and cleaning up after them. It was a dirty job but it suited them well. Francis was all too willing to serve, and when the boat pulled away from the dock later that day, he knew they were one step closer to their destiny.

"Brother Leo, I want to give you your prayer for the day," Francis said as he scrubbed a large black pot later that night.

They were sitting on the edge of the deck where they could wash the kitchen waste into the open sea, and the moon shone brightly above their heads. "'Where there is darkness, bring your light.' This is such an important prayer Leo, for it reveals the real essence of the journey we are on. Look at our dear Sister Moon who reflects the light of Brother Sun, illuminating the path we walk, even the deck of this ship where we work. When she hides behind the dark clouds we stumble and fall upon the rocky ground, unable to see even the smallest stone that would block our way. But when she is bright, when she opens her arms to embrace and reflect the sun, then the sky itself sings for joy and we walk safely toward the Gates of Holiness. In the same way we are meant to reflect the Light of God which lives within us now, and in doing so we become the vehicle through which darkness is dispelled."

"And what of these men who are on board with us today but tomorrow are off to fight and kill?" Leo asked. "How can we give this Light to those who are weighted down with the heavy armor of hatred and violence?"

"Look at the moon," Francis said as he laid his brush on the deck and rose to the side of the ship. "She will teach you everything you need to know about the Light of God. Brother Sun is hidden from our sight, off to another part of the world to shed his light, but he sends his little sister to reflect his radiance and love till he returns. Sister Moon can also teach us the blessed grace of humility. She does not boast and claim to be the Light, but holds perfectly still and allows herself to be used by the Light. We too are called to be used by God, like a broom that sits in the corner of the room. The broom can do nothing on its own, but when it surrenders to the one who knows the truth, then it sweeps and cleans the whole house.

"Or think of the lute that sits in the corner waiting for the master musician to lay his hands upon its neck, then stroke the strings till it sings. The lute is quiet on its own and sings only in the silent memory of its dreams. But when it surrenders, only then do the strings vibrate and a song comes forth to sooth even the most hardened among us."

Just then a crusader walked noisily up the wooden steps, then fell onto the deck with his arms and legs spread wide. It was clear to Francis and Leo that he was drunk, caught up in the ruckus taking place below. The soldier lifted his head from the floor and noticed the two friars looking at him.

"What are you two looking at?" He cursed in their general direction. "What business do you have looking at me at all? You're just a couple of beggars, probably free-loading your way across these waters, while I am a soldier in the service of God, a Crusader off to kill the infidels."

"We too are soldiers of the Lord," Francis said as he rose and walked over to the man. "Our greatest joy is to follow God's Voice onto the battlefield where hatred seems to rule, and to deliver a message of peace. That is why we are on this boat, to be taken to the Crusades and to do battle with the forces of evil."

"Then you are on your way to fight the Muslims?" the soldier said as he sat up to study the strange man standing in front of him.

"We are off to love the Muslims," Francis said. "Violence begets more violence, while love gives rise to peace and compassion. My brother and I are of a different sort of army than you. We are not bent upon destroying the enemy, but embracing them. We intend to request a private audience with the Sultan of Syria, and once there we will tell him of God's Will."

The man stared at Francis in disbelief, then fell backwards in thunderous laughter.

"What are you saying to me?" the soldier roared. "You must be insane. How could one such as you be allowed to travel beside these brave men?"

"Yes, I am insane," Francis laughed, obviously enjoying the soldier's sour attitude. "I have gone mad with the love of God. But oh, my strong brother, I have learned so very much from this madness. I was once like you, a gallant soldier riding off to war, bent upon death and victory. But now look at me. Brother Sun has illuminated my soul and now I see so clearly. Hatred and violence are not the weapons God prefers, but compassion and love. This is the sword that destroys the vanity that leads to war. Cultivate these virtues and you will be mad like me."

The soldier stopped laughing and tried to focus his eyes on the man he saw. It was as if he was suddenly struck sober, as if something Francis said touched a deep place in his heart. Leo, overwhelmed by what he saw, took the drawing pad out from beneath his tunic and began to sketch the amazing expression he saw on Francis' face when he talked.

"Who are you?" the soldier asked. "You do not speak like any crazy person I have met before. Tell me more about yourself and why you're here."

"I am no one," Francis said, "but there is a Light that has illuminated my soul and I seek only to give that same Light to everyone I encounter. And now it is you who sits before me, and it is to you that I shall offer this great joy. I pray that you feel and will come to know this Light, that it may illumine the dark corners of your heart, teaching you about the peace that surpasses all understanding."

"Ah, why am I listening to you? I must be more drunk than I thought from the wine and the sickening motion of his boat. Or perhaps I should drink more, then you will fade away like a mist before my eyes."

"War is but a mist," Francis said to him in a quiet somber voice. "It promises one thing but always brings another. You think you are fighting for peace, or even honor. These things are illusions, my brother, until we discover the source of all peace and the very well of honor. When you discover that source then you will drop the bucket of your life into this well and pull from its depths living water that will quench your thirst. Until then, as long as you seek peace where it cannot be found, you will be as parched as the desert. Nothing will satisfy you, not even war."

The soldier stood up and just for a moment it seemed as if he understood. Then he shrugged his shoulders and grunted. He turned toward the door and went back to his comrades.

"What do you think he will do?" Leo asked.

"He will drink more wine and hope I was a dream. But in the morning, when he sees me serving him, he will wonder. This is all the Light of God needs, Brother Leo—our wonderment. It means we are ready to consider possibilities which we were closed to a moment before. And like the light that streams into a dark room when the door is opened but a crack, so will the Light of God reveal the truth of our souls when we open just a bit."

Chapter Nine

"Where there is sadness, bring your joy"

y the time the Crusaders woke up and stumbled to their feet, Francis and Leo were already preparing a meal to satisfy their hunger. The heavy pots were filled with various vegetables and meats, while Antonio, the head cook, was busy ordering his workers from one place to another, making sure everything was ready.

"You do not want to see what these soldiers are like if their food is not ready when they want it," Antonio yelled. "They will tear this ship apart, then none of us will make it to the other side."

"Today we have two jobs," Francis whispered into Leo's ear. "For now we will help to fill the physical hunger these men feel, but later we will have a much more important opportunity. Later we will help fill what their souls hunger for, a hunger they perhaps do not recognize, but which is there nonetheless."

The soldiers were loud and rude. Some seemed as if they were still drunk from the previous night, while others were white from the constant swaying of the ship. Now and then one of the Crusaders grabbed Francis' arm, yelling for him to fill his plate or cup. He never once lost his smile but willingly met their requests, giving them everything they asked for.

After some time Leo came across the soldier they had met the previous night. The man didn't seem to recognize him at first, but when Leo leaned over to pour water into his cup he sat back and took a closer look.

"Wait," the soldier said, "you were with that other beggar I saw last night. Oh, how I prayed you were a dream. I spent half the night tossing his silly words around my head. Where is that little man, the one who filled my brain with such foolish notions?"

"He is over there," Leo said, pointing to Francis.

The soldier pushed back from the table and clumsily made his way to the corner where Francis served. Leo thought he saw a flash of anger in his eye, but the closer the man came to the saint the more it dissolved into fear.

"What have you done to me?" the soldier asked, grabbing Francis by the sleeve of his habit.

"Good morning, my strong friend. I'm so happy to see you again."

"You won't be happy if you don't answer my question. What right do you have to fill my mind with such pious nonsense when I'm drunk and unable to judge things properly? What if my lack of sleep deadens my abilities and I'm killed by the infidels? Is that what you do, keep unsuspecting soldiers like me up so we're easy prey?"

"I intended to make you easy prey for God," Francis said, as if he was playing a game.

"Come with me," the soldier yelled, pulling him up the stairs and onto the deck. Other soldiers followed, for they thought they were about to see a man be thrown overboard. Leo scrambled up behind the crowd till he was finally at Francis' side. If Francis was going to die, he thought, then he would most assuredly be cast over the side of the boat with him.

"I should throw you to the waves," the soldier screamed. "Who are you to tell me…"

"…how to serve God?"

"Yes… how to serve God," the man said, stumbling over his words. "What right do you have to…"

"…reveal to you the Love of God?"

"The Love of God?" the man said as he released his grip. "What does this have to do with…"

"Everything regards the Love our Divine Parent has for us," Francis said as he stepped back to address the whole crowd. "We are here for one reason and one reason only, and that is to learn about God's Love for us, then to give that same love to one another. We are asked to 'Love as God Loves.' Do you see that?

You men are off to fight for Holy Mother Church, and to kill in the name of God. But is this truly the Mind of our Lord? Did he not tell us to love our enemies and do good to those who hate us? And what better way to treat those whose hearts are filled with hate than to embrace them with the Love of God. Imagine the victory you brave men could win if you followed Christ's words in this way."

"But they are infidels," a soldier yelled. "They are the enemies of the Church."

"If that be so then I beg you enter this battle with the sharpest sword you can find," Francis continued. "Go into your armory and pick from that great room a weapon that is sharp enough to render the Muslims helpless. Yes, when they see you approach with this weapon, they will be confounded, knowing not in which direction to run. You will not need to shed a single drop of blood, for they will sense the lightning speed with which they will be undone, and they will surrender to you without a blow."

"What is this sword you speak of?" the first soldier asked, the one they had met the night before.

"It is joy," Francis said, "the joy that springs from the Love of God. Do you not see that the only way to win a war is to employ that which is its opposite? Hatred and war spring from a single source—fear. There can be no other source but this. And what is the antidote to this terrible disease of the soul, the plague that has rendered us helpless in its face? It is love. Fear gives birth to hatred, and from that rocky soil no flower can grow, only sadness. But love, oh yes, my brothers, love is like a rich plot of land that will nourish your soul. In this ground we plant the roots of compassion, and from that holy vine will grow the fruit of joy. When we eat this fruit it will dispel all hatred and fear, and then this war will be like a dream to us, a shadow that is forgotten once the Light has come."

"You make it seem so simple," the soldier said. "But it is not simple at all. Here we are, brave men suited with the finest armor, cast against other men with different ideas and codes of honor. We are so different…"

"No, my brother… that is where you are wrong," Francis interrupted. "You are not different at all. God's Love falls upon us like the rays of holy Brother Sun. He does not judge who is worthy of the Light, but bestows it on everyone who asks. This is what I mean when I say that we must 'Love as God Loves.' Fear sees everything as different and alone, while Love perceives us as one family, a single extension of our Creator. It is ours to imitate Love, not fear. Are we not blessed in the eyes of God when we strive to be like God?

"So I leave you brave soldiers with a single prayer, and I pray you will breathe these words into your hearts that they may transform your lives and reveal to you the true Will of God. And you, Brother Leo, pay close attention, for this will be your prayer today. Say to God only this: 'Where there is sadness, bring your joy.' Then will you be used by the Sword of Love which cuts away the ropes of fear. You have been bound too long, my friends. Is it not now time for you to know the truth?"

Leo thought that the men would storm around his friend and cast him over the side of the boat. They suddenly became loud and rushed toward Francis, but their arms were not hammers that would crush him. They instead crowded around the saint, imploring that he speak more about this love that conquers fear. And Francis did as they asked, preaching for hours about the fire that had engulfed his soul. Leo, in the meantime, sat back against the wall and continued to sketch the portrait he was employed to complete.

Chapter Ten

"Divine Master, grant that I may not seek to be consoled as to console"

he next morning Leo awoke to find Francis sitting a few feet away smiling at him. It was a look Leo had seen many times before, whenever Francis would break through the walls of fear into the expansiveness of love. It had become his home, his refuge, and he rarely retreated into the cave of doubt. This holy state was so natural for Francis, and it was this more than anything that Leo sought to cultivate within himself.

"Brother Leo, I have been thinking about something." Francis said these words while sitting atop a pile of earth that was alongside the road where they had stopped for the night. The ship had arrived in a small town the previous evening and since they had already filled themselves with the leftover food from the boat, there had been no need to beg for their evening meal. They were tired and had walked to the very edge of the town, where they had curled up in a ditch beside the road to sleep.

"We have spoken a great deal about, 'Seeing as God sees,' and 'Loving as God loves,'" Francis continued. "I believe that this is the real essence of the path we walk. Just as our Blessed Lord said, 'Don't you see that you are like gods?' What could he have meant but that we must strive to be in the Mind of God, to learn to think, act and speak just as God?"

"But how are we to do such a thing?" Leo asked him. "We are weak humans, not gods. Isn't it blasphemy to consider ourselves in this light?"

"As I see it, Brother Leo, we have a choice between two ways of seeing. The first is to 'See as God sees,' and to live in the Light of Love. The second is to 'See as God doesn't see,' and to live in the shadow of the fear. The first is like opening your eyes and sensing what has always been in front of you. Love is perceived directly, not imagined or obscured. The second way is like living with your eyes closed. Even if the Beloved were standing by your side, you would be blind to Her Holy presence. You would instead imagine dark shapes and shadowy figures which seek to destroy your life. You would not perceive reality, but the shadow of reality which frightens you and forces you deeper into fear."

Leo tried to understand these words, but it was so different from the way he was raised. Like the men they had sailed across the sea with, he had been taught that it was sane to strive after what is good, and to destroy anyone who sought to pervert such order. And from a religious perspective, it is holy and blessed to accept one's human fate and not seek to rise above what has rightly been bestowed. It is likewise a grievous sin to seek the Mind of God, for such a mind is beyond our comprehension, beyond the reach of our scattered nature.

Francis seemed to read Leo's thoughts, and so he stood up and walked over to his friend's side.

"Tell me what you think of God," Francis asked.

"I don't understand. Do you want me to tell you who I think God is, or how God behaves?"

"Tell me anything you wish, my brother. I want to know how you perceive this one that we have surrendered our lives to."

Leo stood up and paced back and forth for a moment, deep in thought. Then he turned toward Francis and said: "God is the essence of holiness."

"And what is holiness?" Francis asked.

"Well, holiness is what God is. It is the nature of goodness which defines God."

"And now tell me about goodness."

"Goodness is the opposite of evil," Leo said. "It is the state of being in favor with God."

"One final question, Leo: What is evil?"

"Evil is... it is the opposite of God... being out of favor with God."

Francis smiled and turned around, then walked slowly away from his friend. Leo was confused and wondered if he had said something wrong, something which had offended the saint. He walked fast so that he caught up with his friend within seconds.

"Tell me, Francis, have my words angered you in some way?"

Francis turned around and put his hand on Leo's left shoulder. "Oh no, not at all. I was just thinking."

"Tell me then, what is in your mind now?"

Francis turned back around and pointed to the beautiful landscape that stretched out before them. To the left was a wide valley with trees and flowers all abloom. It seemed to stretch for miles, and the morning sun danced across the grass like tiny diamonds radiant and wet. To the right was the sea with its distant waves washing over the heavy rocks. Each of these scenes were so different, and yet they came together in a dance of harmony and grace.

"Look at this incredible sight," Francis said to Leo. "The land and the sea feel so different when they embrace our earthly form. If you were to lie down in that field and roll in the grass, you would rise covered in dirt and flowers, and you would smell like the earth. And if you were to dive into the waves that lap against the shore, then swim out until you are tired, you would return cold and wet, smelling like the salt that hardens against your skin. Yes, it is clear that these two are different in how they appear and how they feel, but these differences seem to fade when you stand where we are now, gazing upon them both as if they are one."

"I don't understand," Leo said with confused eyes.

"I asked you those questions just now to show you your own mind. Holiness, goodness, evil... these are all ideas, concepts which separate you from reality. God is not a thought, Leo. God is an experience that transcends thought. You can stand here staring at the sea which is miles away and wonder how it feels to dive into its cold embrace. And yet, such a thought will never reveal the experience you seek. You must run toward the ocean, strip naked and throw yourself into the sea... then you will know how it feels to swim, not in your imagination, but with your whole self.

"Now let's speak for a moment about the Vision of God," he continued. "When God looks out across this expanse as we are doing now, He does not say: 'There is the ocean and there is the land... see how different they are?' She says, 'There is God and there is God... see how they are the same?' When you experience the reality that lies behind your thoughts, my brother, then you will see everything as the same, as one with the Mind of God. Then you will understand what it means to 'See as God sees.'"

"But how can God see everything as the same?" Leo asked. "There are those in the world who are good and those who are evil. Some people bend their lives around the vice of sin, while others entwine their souls around the root of love. How can we all be the same, and how can God look past these differences?"

"This is for God to reveal to you, not me. I can only point out the path that leads to your home. You are the one who must journey its distance. Along the way many things will be revealed to you, many lessons that will teach you about the Mind of the Beloved. If you embrace that vision, then you will race toward the destination you seek. If you resist that vision, then you will wander aimlessly through the forest seeking the path that would lead you to safety. No, this is not something you can study with your mind, but a reality you must experience with your heart."

"Then show me this path, Francis. I desire only the experience you speak of, the Light that leads to the Gates of Heaven. I have cast aside everything the world holds dear and have claimed for myself only the vision you behold. Tell me what I have to do, and I will accomplish it with joy."

"Very well," Francis said to him. "Over the next three days I will give you a prayer that will reveal the vision you seek. Remember that you always have a choice—to perceive the world love would show, or fear. Each of these three prayers will make clear this choice, and will lead you into one of two worlds, one where the Light of God reveals all things, the other that is shrouded in darkness."

Francis motioned for Leo to kneel with him on the ground. Then they joined hands and Francis said: " 'Divine Master, grant that we may not seek to be consoled as to console.' This is your prayer, Brother Leo. We will walk in silence today as you allow the Vision of God to reveal its secrets to your open mind."

hey had been walking for several hours without saying a word. Now and then Francis would look over at Brother Leo and bless him with a gentle smile. Leo's face was focused and tight as if the wheel of his mind was spinning out of control. This was not at all what Francis had in mind. Rather, he had hoped Leo would simply open his eyes to the lessons that were all around him, all the gentle reminders that bless the ordinary world. The trees, the birds, and most especially the creatures of the earth that scurried about near their feet... they all had something to teach about compassion. Francis realized that this was the single lesson he would have Leo learn—the true meaning of compassion. Were he to learn to this, then the secrets of Heaven would surely be revealed to him.

"Leo, I think I have made a mistake," Francis said as he stopped, breaking the silence. "I'm afraid I have removed from today's prayer the most important ingredient: Joy."

"I don't understand," Leo said. "How does joy..."

"Oh, joy is a most important tool. Without it the lessons I would give would be like biting into a sour piece of fruit. It would surely satisfy your hunger, but you would not be anxious for your next meal. I realize now that I shouldn't make these lessons so serious. It is better to learn the art of compassion with a smile than with a hard, studied face."

"You have never mentioned the art of compassion before, Brother Francis. Tell me more about this."

"Well, today's prayer is all about compassion. 'Grant that I may not seek to be consoled as to console.' This is a rather strange idea unless we understand the subtle nature of truth which has as its foundation a single lesson—'The Lord our God is One.' Jesus also told us that he is the vine and we are the branches. Can anyone separate the root from the trunk, the trunk from the branch, or the branch from vine? Each one extends from the other making a whole organism that we call a tree. What can this mean but that we are One with the Oneness of God?

"And if this be true, if we are not separate from each other just as we are not separate from God, then anything we do, everything that we give, is received by us the instant it is given. What we do to another, no matter how distant they appear, we do to ourselves. Whenever we give to another, regardless of the cost, we give to ourselves. Realize this truth, my dear brother, and you will realize the gifts of Divine Compassion."

"And so the prayer you have given to me," Leo said, "means that I should give what I think I need? If I feel the need for consolation then I should offer it to another, for that is the only way to realize the truth?"

"Once again, Brother Leo, I can only point my finger toward the truth. It is up to you to seize the experience."

The two men looked to the side of the road and noticed the figure of someone sleeping beneath a tree. Francis, as if he was suddenly overwhelmed with joy, ran to the tree and grabbed hold of a branch that was a few feet above the man. Then he began swinging back and forth, his feet nearly kicking the one who slept, and he started singing a song he was clearly making up for the occasion.

"Oh, show me the road that leads to joy... I am your servant, Lord... your little boy. Help me to realize the path we walk... that I may do your will instead of talk."

The man suddenly woke up to find Francis swinging a few inches away from his chest, and he pulled himself a good distance away where he would be safe from this crazy man.

"What the devil!" the man said. "What are you doing? Didn't you see me sleeping here?"

"But it is the middle of the day," Francis said as he jumped down from the branch. "Are you not needed in the Master's vineyard, or required to build the sacred temple that is falling to ruin?"

"I am sleeping here because I am depressed," the man said as he gathered his things into a sack. "All my friends have gone off to fight some holy battle, and I have been left behind to wallow in self-pity."

Leo took a step backwards and he seemed as if afraid to come any closer to the man. When Francis saw this, he walked over to Leo and said, "Brother Leo, this man is depressed, and so he seeks our counsel. Join me at his side and we will help him perceive the Light."

But Leo refused to take a step in the man's direction, and acted as if he was suddenly struck with fear. Francis walked back over to the man and sat down at his side.

"Dear brother, I am sorry to hear that your friends have deserted you. Perhaps they are not as far away as they seem. Tell me, sir, do you live somewhere near here?"

"I live just up the road in Assisi," he said. "There has been a plague in my town and it has claimed the hearts of many young soldiers. The young Francesco Bernadone has seduced them all, and they have retreated to the caves and hills to pray, leaving me to sit in despair."

Francis stood up again and walked over to Leo who was by now as white as a ghost.

"What is happening here?" Leo demanded. "What sort of trickery is this? You know very well who this is. It is our friend, Renato, my closest comrade before I left Assisi. And yet he does not recognize either one of us... and he says that Assisi..."

"Brother Leo, this is a fellow pilgrim who needs our love. Would you deny him the consolation he seeks?"

"Francis," Leo said, "my heart has ached for Renato for many years. When I left my family to follow your example, I did not shed a single tear. And when I left Assisi, leaving behind the great stone walls that saw my birth, I never once looked back in sorrow. But I have never been able to forget him, the man who sits a few feet from us now. We left him behind, all his brothers and friends, and he cursed us and has despised us since. It has been like an ulcer that eats away at my soul. How is it possible..."

"Why do you question the moment of your healing?" Francis asked him. "Go to him and explain. He will not recognize you. See what balm you can apply to his wound, and you will discover a truth within yourself that has eluded you till now."

Leo stepped away from Francis as if he was unsure of his next move. Was this an apparition or a ghost he saw, the shadowy projection of his own hidden mind? What he saw was impossible. This could not be his friend, Leo thought to himself, but a man whose face stirred a memory he had hidden from for years. Maybe he imagined the words he heard, about Assisi and Francesco Bernadone. Leo began to gather his courage and took a long step forward till he stood a few feet away from the man.

"Greetings, dear Sir, my name is Leo...Brother Leo. Do you recognize me?"

The man stood up and looked at Leo. He was dirty and his clothes were like rags, but when Leo looked into his eyes he knew who it was. The dirt and clothes could not hide truth from him. It was most definitely Renato, the friend he left behind a decade earlier.

"No, I've never seen you before," Renato said. "But you should tell your friend to be careful where he swings. He would have fallen on top of me if I hadn't moved."

Leo looked over at Francis who was by now sitting on a rock beside the road. Whatever was happening, whatever was the source of this mystery, it was for Leo alone.

"I heard you say that your friends were gone and you are now alone," Leo said. "I understand how you feel, for I can remember a time when I behaved in a similar fashion, leaving behind a friend who was a true companion. For years I have carried this wound, and so I am grieved to hear about your bad luck."

"Why did you leave your friend behind?" Renato asked. "Could you not have brought him along on any adventure... that is, if he really was the comrade you say?"

"Oh, I tried," Leo said. "I tried to share my joy with him, the way God touched my soul and opened my eyes. But he would not follow the path I walked and chose to stay behind. How I wished he would have come to visit our little home to see the simplicity of our lives. Maybe then he would have changed his mind and opened his heart to his brothers."

"Why haven't you gone to him?" Renato asked. "Why wait for your friend to move when your feet are as sure as his? Perhaps that is all he needs, a single glance that would release him from his fear."

Francis watched the two men who were by that time sitting together beneath the tree. They talked for a long time but Francis did not need to hear their words to know what was happening. Then he noticed that the sun was about to fall behind the distant hills, and he knew the dream he had created was about to end. He stood up and motioned to Leo that it was time to leave.

The two men stood looking at each other for a long moment, and their eyes conveyed more than words ever could. Then Leo wrapped his arms around Renato and said goodbye. He walked back to Francis who had already started up the road.

"It seemed as if he appreciated your consolation," Francis said to him. "And your own heart, yes, something has changed there as well. Isn't it interesting that you would offer a gift to someone when you yourself required the same healing?"

"Yes, it is interesting." And that was all Brother Leo said, for the strange dream had left a sudden impact on his life. What more could he say? The lesson had found its mark.

Chapter Eleven

"Grant that I may not seek to be understood, as to understand"

eo's feet were beginning to feel the sharp rocks of the road more acutely than ever before. He had not owned a real pair of shoes for many years, ever since he cast away the worldly fashions that had chained him to his former life. It was not the world he clung to now, but the earth itself. This was one of the finest lessons he had learned from Francis, the difference between the riches of the world and the sheltering embrace of the Mother. One was a chain and the other was the key, and the brothers continuously sought the freedom of a life lived close to the ground.

"One cannot fall far from the Grace of God when one lives so close to the Mother," Francis would often say. "Our feet are firmly rooted in her heart, but her strong arms lift us to the Heavens where our souls can fly. It is far better to be poor in the eyes of men but rich in the sight of God. This is why we live like this, free from the traps and snares of lofty desires. Let your feet rub against her, my brothers, as if each step is a prayer of gratitude for the bountiful gifts she bestows upon us all."

Leo's feet had rubbed against the rocky soil more than he wished that particular day, and he wondered if this discomfort was really part of their vow to simplicity. Maybe a pair of worn out sandals would suffice, on one hand honoring the simple lifestyle he loved, and on the other hand, or foot, giving him a moment's comfort. It made him laugh when he imagined Francis in this way, and just for a moment he forgot his pain and remembered why he began this journey.

And yet, Francis was always attentive, and he noticed the way Leo was limping along. Then he remembered his own youth and the fine garments he once wore, and just for a moment he found himself longing for the warmth of his former home with his mother watching him from the chair and his father off in the corner counting the money he had earned during the day in the family shop. Francis never once complained about the way he was raised, but everything changed when he was struck with a Divine fever. And just as St. Paul had been thrown from his horse, Francis' eyes were suddenly and permanently opened. The old world was gone and was replaced by a life of dirt, hunger and uncertainty. But, oh, how he loved that simple life. Now and then a memory surfaced that drew his attention, but then he remembered the lady he had chosen as his own, Lady Simplicity, and he opened his arms to her.

"Leo, why don't we stop for awhile and rest? You have hardly opened your pad for days and we don't want to return to Assisi without something to show the other brothers. I pray only that you be merciful with your pencil and look beneath this dirt and skin to who I really am."

"I draw less what I see with my eyes and more of what my heart beholds," Leo said to Francis. "And yet, if it were the dust that defined us, then you and I would be very rich indeed."

"You see Leo, you have already been filled with the wisdom of our Blessed Lord. It is through the eyes of God you have seen me, not through the eyes of the flesh which see nothing as it truly is. God sees only the good in us and disregards these earthly vessels. They are here one moment and gone the next, not even the blink of an eye in eternity. But our soul, yes, this is what God loves, and when we love in this way then we begin to see the truth; we 'See as God sees.' We come back to this one thought again and again because it is the very foundation of the peace you seek. Continue to see in this way, my dear brother, and Heaven will be yours, not when you die, for death proclaims love as unreal, but here and now, the only time there is in truth."

"You speak of these things and I am filled with wonder," Leo said. "My heart rejoices when I hear your words, but my mind rebels. It cannot understand for it makes no sense from the perspective I hold. How can I 'See as God sees' when I am but a mortal man? Would I not need to be in the Mind of God to know such vision, and if I consider such a thing, am I not a blasphemer?"

"Some day you will understand that the Mind of God is the only thing that is real," Francis said to him. "But for now open your eyes and draw what you see in front of you. Then I will speak to you more of this mystery."

Francis sat down on a large rock and Leo took his pad from under his arm. Then Leo fastened his gaze upon the face of his brother and tried to forget all the ways he was accustomed to 'seeing.' How many times had he heard Francis tell him that the physical eyes do not see anything at all, save that which grows cold and dies in the end? Francis' whole life was focused on seeing everyone he encountered as holy, looking past all human imperfection to the well of grace that defines the Truer Self. Could Leo capture such a face on his drawing pad? Or should such a task be left for the angels who draw not upon earthly paper but upon the souls of each one of us?

Francis could feel his brother's confusion and said to him: "Brother Leo, your prayer today should help you see past these questions that engage your mind. Focus your mind on these words: 'Lord, grant that I may not seek to be understood, as to understand.' You believe it is impossible to perceive the Mind of God, as if you were but a creature without need to ascend to the throne of holiness. We are here for one reason and it is to 'See as God sees.' Earlier I said that God sees everything as the same while we see everything as separate and distinct..."

"But everything is separate and distinct," Leo said to him. "You and I are in different bodies and we live different lives. Tell me, then, how are we the same?"

"We are the same in one thing only, Leo, and yet this is the most important thing in the world. We are the same in Holiness. God sees us as the same because only grace flows from the Mind of God. We look around and we see sin, division and war. God looks past these illusions and sees only the truth. What is the truth, then? Simply this: Who you are, the truth in you, cannot change because the Mind of God cannot change. It is and will always be whole and perfect. Therefore, everything that extends from God is whole and perfect as well."

"But what of sin?" Leo asked. "Surely God does not claim this part of us. I cannot understand how we are to look past these things that are decayed and corrupt."

"Seek not to understand, Leo, but to be understood by God. This statement seems to oppose the prayer I gave you today, does it not? And yet, it is only when you are understood by God that you grasp the more profound understanding that eludes the intellect. You are trying to use your mind to understand what appears only to the heart. Your intellect is very much like your physical eyes, it perceives only what you allow it to perceive. And if you have built a world of dreams and have made those dreams seem real, then how can you perceive the deeper reality which your mind and eyes cannot comprehend at all? God asks us to claim for ourselves the Vision of Holiness that is eternal, not the world that is here one minute, but then disappears with a single breath of air. Then we will see further than physical eyes were meant to see and perceive a world where peace, grace and unconditional love are not contradicted in any way."

Leo put the pad on the ground for it was impossible for him to draw at all with such confusing thoughts. "Brother Francis, you know that I love you and honor everything I have learned on this journey. But I can no longer listen to such ideas for they seem to contradict everything we have been taught before this. There are those in the world who do good, and these people should be rewarded for their acts of charity. And there are others who seek to destroy what is good, and these people deserve to be punished for their actions. How can God look past the things which harm the ones who turn their hearts toward mercy?"

Then Francis stepped up to his brother and kicked him as hard as he could in his leg. Leo stumbled to his feet and after grabbing the aching spot said in a loud voice: "Why have you assaulted me in this way? Have my words offended you so much that..."

"You have committed a terrible sin against me," Francis said as he sat back down on the rock, "and the punishment you have received was well deserved."

"But what have I done to deserve such a thing?" Leo asked. "I have only asked you to help me understand..."

"Last night while I was asleep I dreamed that you and I were walking down the road together," Francis said to him in a gentle tone. "Suddenly, without warning, you struck me on the side of the head, and I fell to the ground in agony. The blow was enough to wake me from my sleep. And now that we are here and I have remembered this sin, I have decided to pay you back for your attack."

"But it was only a dream," Leo said to him as he rubbed his sore leg. "Why am I being punished for something I did to you while you were dreaming? The offense never took place while I was awake, but at night as I lay sleeping at your side. Is it reasonable to punish someone for a dream that you created in your own mind?" He stopped and grew somber. "Alas, you spoke of this before, how our lives are lived like men dreaming and our misdeeds vanish in the mind of God. It seems I did not learn my lesson. You were right to kick me."

"You have answered well for yourself," Francis said as he walked over to his brother. "When we understand the difference between what occurs in a dream and what occurs in reality, then the Vision of God will be ours. God is One, Brother Leo, and we are One in God. Anything that forces us to be separate and isolated is nothing but a dream, and at no time can such a dream exist in the Mind of God. Therefore, no punishment is required for an offense that never occurred in truth, just as you said to me. So I am sorry for the pain in your leg, my friend, but that pain will be as nothing if it helps you see the truth that cannot be ignored by our Beloved. If it is understanding you seek, then learn to 'See as God sees,' and the dream of separation will end on its own."

Leo wondered if he should say something, but no words came to him. And yet he understood exactly what had happened, not with his mind, but with his heart. He picked up his drawing pad, placed it under his arm, and followed Francis on the journey.

Chapter Twelve

"Lord, grant that I may not seek to be loved, as to love"

here was no way for Francis and Leo to know when they actually crossed into the Muslim territory. There were no signs, no warnings, only the subtle shift that quickened their hearts and filled them with a strange anticipation. Francis could feel his destiny calling him and he would not ask it to wait.

How many Crusaders had they passed along the way who warned them of their fate if they continued this insane quest? The Muslims are barbaric, they said, and would not take lightly this assault, no matter how well intended. They would be tortured and killed if they were captured, and the great mission they had undertaken would end in despair. Better to preach to the brave men who defend the faith, said they, than waste such pearls upon the Godless lot beyond the saving grace of mercy.

And each time he heard such talk, Francis would smile and nod appreciatively. Then he and Leo would leave their company and continue on, not dissuaded from their holy goal. Upon his lips there was always a blessing for the men they met, but there was a still deeper voice he saved for the Sultan and his people.

"Let this be your prayer today," Francis said to Leo as they continued along a winding path. "'Grant, oh Lord, that I may not seek to be loved, as to love.' Do you see how these last three days have prepared us for the final test ahead? We have not sought to be consoled, or understood, or even loved, but have seen that we are filled only as we give these virtues to another. There is no difference at all between the soldiers we leave and the ones we seek, just as there is no difference between you and me. In the eyes of God we are all holy, and God's radiance is One. Would that we sought this sight above all things and saw everyone through these Blessed Eyes. Surely grace would follow such vision and this war would melt in the face of such grandeur."

They then came around a sharp bend in the path and saw a man standing in the middle of the road spinning round and round as if in a trance. Though Francis and Leo stood only a short distance away, the man did not seem to notice them but continued turning like a spinning top, one hand pointing down toward the earth and the other toward the sky. The two friars watched him in amazement, for no matter how long he turned, he did not lose his balance and fall. And with each rotation they could see a look in his eyes that was sweeter than anything Francis could think of. The love of God reflected off this dervish like fire, and Francis began dancing in the center of the road alongside the man.

Then as suddenly as it began, the two men stopped, and as if well rehearsed, they bowed toward one another in holy reverence. Leo stood back and watched for he knew something marvelous was taking place in front of his eyes. Francis and the dervish slowly raised their heads until their eyes locked, and just for an instant the world stopped turning to pay homage.

Something happens when twin souls meet that the world cannot understand. There is a flame which after being passed from one candle to another forgets for a moment the original source of the fire. Now and then these candles meet and the memory of the original flame is reignited, and the fire leaps forward in recognition. In the whole history of the world there are but a few instances when this has occurred, when two people from the same fire burst forward and remember the spark that made them. This was one such occasion.

Finally Francis found his voice and said: "Greetings from the God of Life, holy dervish. What fire is this I see burning in your eyes that ignites a still deeper fire in my heart? Is this a mirror I see before me, a magic glass that reflects not the contours of my face but the radiance of my soul? It is as if I have traveled to a distant land, far away from my home, to meet myself on this road. Tell me, what is your name and how may I serve you, for in serving you I give glory to the Beloved."

The dervish smiled and said: "My name is Maulana Rumi, friar. Your eyes fool you, as physical eyes so often do, for it is not my face nor my spirit you behold but the face of the Beloved that looks upon us both and smiles. You who have plunged into that Holy Chamber and drowned in that infinite ocean of light, where on this earth will you go and not perceive me? For I am no one at all, and we disappear together in the gentle waves that flow from our lover's heart. We are her toys, her playthings, but to us she is the womb of life, and from that womb are we born again."

There was a long silence between them, and Leo wondered if they had abandoned words altogether for the sake of the deeper song which human lips can never sing. Angels have ears to hear such sounds since they are not fooled by the meaningless rambling that so often passes for speech. They hear the spaces that exist between words, and they live in the infinite possibility of those spaces. Were it not for Leo walking toward them and breaking the spell, Francis and Rumi may have never moved from that spot again.

"I can feel the grace of this joining," Leo said, "and I bow before the single heart that beats within two bodies."

Francis blinked his eyes as if waking from a dream, then he stepped closer to Rumi, saying: "Tell me, Holy One, where is it you travel to that we may walk beside you for awhile?"

"A man who does not exist goes nowhere at all," Rumi said. "A handful of salt dissolves into a glass of water and thus one cannot say which is the water and which is the salt. So do we dissolve into the heart of the Beloved, and thus we become the Beloved, losing the former self that was but a shadow compared to this. We will walk together, then, in whatever direction you travel. It matters not whether we move toward or away from the setting sun for it is born anew each day, just as each breath we breathe is a new life to live."

Rumi joined the friars and continued on down the road. Francis explained their quest, all about their desire to speak to the Sultan and explain the deeper pulse of Jesus' message. Rumi seemed genuinely moved by Francis' words and stopped suddenly in the road. A single tear fell from his eye, and Leo thought once again how similar he was to his brother. Francis walked over to Rumi and put his hand on his shoulder saying:"Tell me what your inner vision beholds that I may weep with you."

"When I was young I was raised to embrace Allah and defend the holy precepts of Islamic law. But then the Beloved inflamed my heart and I discovered the higher law from which all things proceed. There is no law, religious or civil, that can eclipse what love reveals, for love's lesson is one: 'That which I give to thee is received by me.' I sense that your hearts have already discovered this truth. And so I look past these bodies that seem to separate us for a moment and I behold this law as it moves through us as a mist. Then together we will breathe this vapor into our lungs and hold it there till we have absorbed everything it can teach us. What more can we ask once this heavenly fire has illuminated these sacred forms?"

"This law is the very fire you speak of," Francis said. "What I have claimed for you cannot be removed from my own hand, for there is in truth but one extension of the love and the loveliness of God. Each one of us is but a reflection of that fire, and if we become conscious of the law that giving and receiving are but a single act, then we enter into the stream that draws us into the ocean which dissolves our splintered selves and makes us one again. Then we shall look out upon the world we behold and say:

'When I am hungry,

Give me someone I can feed.

And when I am thirsty,

Give me someone to get a drink for.'

Then will our hunger be filled and our thirst satisfied, not with earthly food or drink but with the Light that flows from the Beloved into our open mouths."

"You both speak of the Beloved as if she were with us now," Leo said to them. "Tell me as much as you can about this maiden that I may pursue her with the same abandon as you."

Rumi laughed out loud and began running in circles like a madman. "How can one describe drunkenness?" he screamed. "The fire that fills a man's head when he drinks and the unsteady motion of his step can never be described to a person whose lips have never tasted wine. And what of the woman who suddenly sees with her eyes the man she has beheld but in her dreams? Can words make you feel her heart which beats faster every time he looks in her direction? It would be better for you to hold perfectly still and not say a word lest the movement of your own heart be disturbed. Words are but symbols of symbols and can never approach the holy altar where lovers lay down their lives and sacrifice their dreams for a single moment of rapture. You can never approach the Beloved in this way, for she will come to you as she wills, just as you feel the wind blowing but you can never direct its course."

"Speak to me more of this fire," Francis said with equal enthusiasm, "for your words spark the memory of my lover's voice which called me away from the world of form into her formless embrace. You speak with the same cadence as she, as if we were tutored together in her bed. And as you have said, her law bids us to pursue not her love, but to give the love we seek, not to beg for her sheltering embrace, but to embrace all, and to know that each person we extend our arms to and draw close to our breast is really the Beloved in disguise."

"So she is nowhere and everywhere at the same time?" Leo queried.

"The person who drinks a single glass of wine is willing to share the effects of its bouquet with anyone who asks," Rumi said, "while the one who drinks the whole bottle attempts to describe the feeling but his words are slow and halting. And what of the person who swims in an ocean of wine, whose whole being has been absorbed into its drunken embrace? Are they able to describe what they feel, or do they look up over the waves of that ocean with eyes that comprehend what speech cannot?

"I tell you, friar, when the Beloved claims you, be very careful, for she is a most jealous lover. There is no thought that can equal her grace, and if you dare to think about another, then she will flee from your bed till you come crawling back to her. Such is the love that surpasses everything the world holds dear."

"My dearest brother," Francis said to Leo, "you have asked a good question and you deserve an answer. The Beloved is indeed everywhere you look, yet nowhere at all. If you beseech her counsel with a heart that is open then her love will flow from every direction you look, from every person you perceive. This is the true meaning of the prayer I gave you today. It is in your willingness to give love to everyone, to see the Beloved in everyone, that calls her to your side. She cannot resist one whose entire life is a song in her honor, who looks around every corner expecting to see her face. Indeed, this person will enjoy her radiance both in the company of a sinner and the presence of a saint. They are the same to her, and so shall it be the same to the ones who love her. Find her in the eyes of whoever is standing in front of you, then surely she will be yours."

"I understand," Leo said. "This is the universal law which unites our hearts with the hearts of all beings. If I perceive that I need anything at all then it is best to give that blessing to another. Then it will surely be mine, for that person is not separate from me at all but intimately linked through the Vision of the Beloved."

"Holy friar," Rumi said, "it is ours to live in this message, ours to sing this song to everyone we meet. Then perhaps we will learn to focus on the ways we are the same rather than the ways we're different. Then perhaps wars like this one which separates lovers of God like us will cease forever."

Rumi traveled with Francis and Leo for the rest of that day, then turned to leave when the sun began its ecstatic dance over the mountain tops. It was like they were saying goodbye to someone they had known their entire lives, so close was the bond. And yet, they knew that there are no real good-byes, for we can never truly leave one another. What our bodies do is of little consequence to hearts that are forever joined.

Chapter Thirteen

"For it is in giving that we receive"

y the time Leo saw the two Islamic soldiers it was too late to stop the terrible scene. Francis was already running toward them with his arms outstretched, and the suddenness of the soldiers' reaction was frightening. One man brought the back of his hand down against the side of Francis' face while the other cracked his skull with the handle of his sword. When Leo arrived, Francis was lying motionless on the ground with blood streaming from his mouth. Then everything went dark, and Leo fell unconscious at his brother's side.

It was impossible to know how many hours had passed. Leo was the first to open his eyes and he sat up in the small cell where they were being held captive and looked around. Francis was rolled up in a ball near the corner, and Leo crawled on his knees till he was with his friend.

"Francis... please wake up," Leo said. The sound was enough to jar Francis from his rough sleep, and before he sat up, he placed both hands against his injured head.

"What has happened to us?" Francis asked. "I feel that my head has been split in half."

"Do you know where we are? Do you remember anything at all about what happened to us?"

"I remember walking," Francis said as he tried to separate the memory from the pain he felt. "Then I remember hearing a sound like a man laughing. As I looked down the road my eyes saw two men, soldiers, but I knew they could not be Christian. My heart leaped within me when I realized these were Muslim soldiers and that the moment of our test had arrived."

"Yes... that is when I noticed them as well," Leo said. "And then I saw you running toward the men, and I saw them deal you a serious blow to the head... the very blow that gives you the pain you now feel."

"And so we are imprisoned," Francis said with excitement as he stood up, nearly striking his head on the low ceiling. "We have been locked inside this cell and now we wait the judgment of the Sultan who is sure to see us. This is the beginning, Brother Leo, but where we end is still a mystery."

"What if this is the end? What if we have been forgotten here, locked away forever in this darkness? Then we will surely fail and this dream of ours will end in sorrow."

"Leo," Francis said placing his hand on his friend's shoulder, "we cannot fail in this, for the door which love has opened can never be shut again by fear. We stand here with our eyes wide, and with ears that hear the sound of the Beloved's call. How could we fail to know the room in which she sleeps when we recognize her voice so easily?"

Then they heard the sound of a large door opening and heavy steps approaching their cell. Francis, who suddenly seemed to forget his pain, put his face against the cold steel bars and tried to see down the dimly lit hall. A man then appeared who had a dark complexion and deep haunted eyes that betrayed no emotion. He held a small wooden club in his hand and hit it against the metal bars to force Francis back into the darkness of the cell.

"Stay away from the bars when I approach the cell," the soldier said in a deep, penetrating voice. "You have been arrested as spies and your fate will soon be decided by the council of judgment. Words and excuses will mean nothing to these men, for your guilt has already been proven and the sentence decided. You will be executed within days, and then we will be done with your kind."

And though the soldier was hard and his heart seemed closed to love, still did Francis reach through those bars, if only in spirit, to caress and befriend him. He stepped close to the bars and said: "Dearest brother, we come to you not as spies, or with any malicious intent at all. We carry in our hearts a message for your great leader, the Sultan of Syria. I pray that you will bring him this request, telling him that two beggars have risked their lives to sing a simple song, a melody that comes straight from the lips of God."

The soldier stared at Francis through the bars and his eyes became like fire. Then he stepped forward so he was no more than a foot away from the saint, and the two men stared at each other for a long time. It was clear to Leo that the soldier meant to do Francis harm, or at least to unleash his fury with words. But Francis' eyes were so filled with Light that the soldier could not remember what he meant to say, and his clenched fist relaxed and fell to his side.

"I will see what I can do. For now relax and I'll have someone bring you some food."

The soldier walked away and closed the heavy door. Leo stood up and walked over to Francis.

"What did you do to him?" Leo asked. "I was sure he was ready to open the door and beat us both. But there was something about the way you looked at him, some magical spell you cast that disarmed him completely. Please tell me what you did so that I may learn how to use this secret force myself."

"There was no magic in my eyes, nor is there a secret force that changed him," Francis said. "All of your lessons have led to this moment, Leo. Everything I have taught you so far has brought you to a single truth, which when you extend to another has the power to melt even the hardest heart. When we began our journey you asked me to teach you the deeper meaning of peace, and each lesson has revealed a different aspect of the peace that surpasses all understanding. But today we enter a new phase of learning, one where every lesson you have learned till now comes together in a single point of Light."

"Tell me, then, about this Light so that this dark cell will not oppress me so."

Francis looked deep into Leo's eyes and said: "Here is the lesson that gives meaning to the rest: 'It is in giving that we receive.' Are you beginning to see how simple the truth is, Leo? If I confronted that man with anger then he would have met me with greater strength, and I hate to think how our fate would have turned. I remembered instead my true desire, for love is my only true quest, and healing is the means to achieve that goal. And so, desiring only love, I gave only love, and you witnessed the result for yourself. How could the soldier hold onto such shadows when Light had so suddenly burst in all around him?"

The huge door opened again and the light from outside streamed into the cell. Francis and Leo could see the silhouettes of two men walking toward them, and when the door closed again they saw the soldier who had been with them before, accompanied by another dressed in an officer's uniform.

"My guard tells me you are both crazy," the officer said, "...that you came here seeking an audience with the Sultan. This is a ploy to escape your execution for we know you're guilty of the crime you've been accused of."

"And what crime is this, sir?" Francis asked.

"You are both Christians and that is enough. Why else would you be in this area if not to spy on our position? You come dressed as common beggars, but beneath your clothes you carry the sword of deceit."

"I explained to your comrade why we have come," Francis said in a gentle voice. "We have a message that is meant for the Sultan's ear, and his alone. We have not come to your country at the request of the Christian force, but against their advice and will. The message we carry could bring a swift end to this war, for it comes from the heart of our Creator."

"And whose Creator is it you speak of?" the officer asked. "The Christian God, or Allah, whom we worship and love?"

"There is only one Creator in all the universe, and it notices no difference between us, regardless of how we choose to address the One God. I worship Allah as you do, for the love of God extends from a single heart and penetrates the dark walls we erect that seem to separate us from one another. We are separate but in our dreams, dear sir, for Allah loves us with equal passion and tenderness."

And just as the soldier had done before him, the officer stared into the bars trying to fathom the peculiar energy he felt coming from the little beggar. As much as he tried, he could not hold onto the feeling of contempt, but watched as his heart began to slowly melt and his anger disappeared. As ridiculous as it seemed, he began to believe that this prisoner held some gift that his great leader might choose to receive.

"There is no telling what your fate will be," the officer said. "But I will at least make the Sultan aware of your presence. If it is his desire to hear your words then we will bring you to the palace where he will judge your message as well as your crime. But if he refuses, then you'll both be taken to the executioner's chamber where you'll breathe your last breath."

The two men turned and walked away from the cell, then opened the door that led to the light. Leo was as amazed as he had been before when he saw how quickly the first soldier changed, but he was starting to understand the true meaning of all the prayers he had been given to study.

"It is all beginning to make sense to me, Francis, all the prayers and lessons I have received since we started our journey together. We began by asking to be made into instruments of peace, like a lute held gently in the hands of our Beloved that sings with a single stroke. I then learned that hatred is but the shadow of love, and it is only when we look past that shadow, passing through it as if it were a cloud, that we see the truth face to face. Then it was as if the whole world began lining up to teach us the lessons of peace, and I began to see how simple truth really is. When I believe I need something, is it not best to give that gift to another? Only then will I realize that I am not separate from that one, but forever united in love. And now here we are, faced with the threat of death, and still we stand in the Light, giving that which is most dear. Love alone has brought us this far, Francis, and regardless of how this journey ends, I have learned everything I can hope to learn in an entire lifetime."

wo days then passed and the friars heard nothing at all. Twice a day a servant brought them a bowl of leftover food and a cup full of water, and it was good to talk to another person, if only for a few moments. But then the servant would leave and they were alone again waiting and praying that their request would be heard.

Leo took this opportunity to continue his portrait, for he did not want to die without it being completed. He often waited for Francis to be deep in prayer, when he was not aware of being watched, and the pencil would flow over the paper with ease. Even if the other friars in faraway Assisi never had the chance to see the completed work, Leo wanted to know he had fulfilled his holy task. Perhaps it was meant for Heaven, he thought to himself, to be hung in some celestial gallery as a symbol of one whose life was a pure reflection of the heart of Christ. Such a thought filled Leo's heart with joy.

Just then they heard the bolt on the large door turn and the officer came down the hall flanked by two guards.

"Your request has been granted," the officer said in a formal tone. "We have come to escort you to the Sultan's palace where you will speak your mind to him. When you are through, you will then be taken from that place to the executioner who will see to your end." Then his voice became soft as if he truly cared about the fate of the friars. "I am sorry it must end like this, for I believe you are holy men. But these are the Sultan's orders, and I am charged to obey."

"Save your sorrow for another hour," Francis said as the guards locked his hands in chains. "You have done us a great service, and we will accept whatever fate the Sultan desires. Do not be fooled by death, my friend, for it is really nothing at all. When you leave a friend in one room and enter into another, your friend does not weep and think that you are gone forever. Raise your voice and they will hear you in the other room. Likewise, if we die today we will still not be beyond reach. Hold me in your heart and I will be at your side again, and you'll hear me whispering into your inner ear. Yes, no matter what happens, we will be fine."

Leo took the drawing pad and placed it beneath his habit, and the two men were taken from their cell.

Chapter Fourteen

"It is in pardoning that we are pardoned"

The palace courtiers shifted nervously from one foot to another as the Sultan screamed in the general direction of his chief adviser.

"It is my decision to toy with the beggars, and I'll not have you questioning my judgment."

"But, your Highness, why waste time with these insignificant men? They wandered into your camp like sheep into a den of wolves. Turn them over to the executioner before they have the chance to pollute our minds further."

"What are you talking about?" the Sultan yelled as he stood up from his chair. "They are harmless wanderers who think they have a message from God. Once and for all I will show these thieves which God is real and which is an illusion."

"There has been disturbing talk amongst the soldiers, your Highness. It seems that these are not ordinary men, but sorcerers. Everyone who has come into contact with them now walks about in a daze and seems ready to abandon this war in favor of peace. What if the rumors are true? What if they were sent here by the Christians to subvert our plans and weaken our intent? Surely it would be wiser..."

"Don't tell me what is wiser. You're dangerously close to losing your own head, so I would be careful how far you push your argument. I want these men standing in front of me and I will be their judge. If they are mad, then I will amuse myself for a while before I have them killed. And if they are as dangerous as you say, then they will learn how the antelope feels the instant the lion severs its jugular. Either way, they are mine to do with as I please."

"Yes, your Highness. I will bring them to you now."

The Sultan sat back in his chair with a look of supreme authority on his face. After all, he had long since proven himself on the battlefield, and he would surely not be frightened by two man dressed in rags, even if they were magicians.

"There is no magic on this earth that can eclipse my courage," he mumbled to himself. "I'll hear their message, then do whatever I want with them."

The huge ornate doors that led into the royal suite slowly opened and the Sultan saw the two men standing barefoot in the entrance. Their appearance was worse then he expected, and yet even from that distance he could sense something rare that seemed to radiate from Francis and Leo, making the rags they wore seem more like fine suits of armor. Francis, on the other hand, looked at the marvelously dressed Sultan and thought for a moment that they were rags he wore, such was the strange energy that passed between the men.

"Don't stand there like fools," the Sultan barked. "Stand before me and deliver your message."

Francis and Leo began the long walk from the door to the Sultan's great chair. It reminded Francis of the first time he stood before the pope and the fear he felt for the first minute or so. But then their eyes met and the fine robes and jewels vanished, and he recognized the pope as a brother. The Sultan's eyes were very much like the man he remembered, but then Francis saw a flash of fire shoot in his direction and he realized that the great test had finally arrived.

"Who do you think you are to request an audience with me?" the Sultan asked them. "You're obviously poor beggars who were probably forced to leave your own land. And now you come to trouble me with your pious proclamations. What makes you think that Allah would use fools to deliver a message to a great king?"

Francis didn't say a word but looked at the Sultan with utter compassion. His chest seemed to grow and expand, as if God was breathing life into his heart. His eyes closed for moment while he said a silent prayer, then looked again at the Sultan and said: "You're right, great one, we are fools and the message we bring to you is foolish as well. In fact, our Master and Lord was also a fool, at least in the eyes of learned men, for his words and deeds made no sense at all to their rational minds. But let me ask you this question, great king. Have you ever been in love?"

The Sultan wasn't sure if he was meant to answer, but he was clearly caught up in the discourse.

"Of course I've been in love, with many women," he said, laughing out loud. "You would do well to remember that I have many wives and each one of them has felt the weight of my love."

"And when you are in love," Francis continued without pause, "did your manner prove rational, or were you like me, a fool dancing for joy without a care in the world? Perhaps your royal subjects looked at you and said, 'What has happened to our king? He behaves like one who is drunk.'"

"No one would dare say such a thing," the Sultan said.

"Yes, I'm sure you are surrounded by loyal servants, but still, you will remember how love possessed you and changed everything you saw."

The Sultan stood looking at Francis and felt a strange feeling overwhelm him. "Yes, I do remember, little man. But what does this have to do with..."

"... the madness I bring?" Francis said. "There is something I want to tell you, great one, that far outweighs the power of every army in the world. I pray that you will entertain my foolishness a moment longer and I will share what I have learned."

The Sultan nodded his head and sat back in his chair. Whatever was happening in front of him, he had an overwhelming desire to see it through to the end. Then he would decide his next move, whether to have the men beheaded as he said before, or spare their lives. It made him feel strong again to remember it was his choice and his alone.

"I want you to understand something that rocked the very foundation of my life," Francis continued. "I was raised to believe that God punishes those who do not follow the path designed by the Christian Church, and it was this very reasoning that led to this terrible war. The Christians believe that their God is the only true God, and before anyone realizes what is happening, we stand together on the open battlefield, sword to sword and blood to blood, till one side or another is left standing. And this is how we decide which God is real.

"What I want to tell you is very simple, great one, and if you have ears to hear these words then you will be as I, a lover of peace. The one whom I call my Master, Jesus of Nazareth, does not agree with the position of my church. He, in fact, preached a gospel that opposes every detail of this war. He said to us: 'Love your enemies, do good to those who hate you, bless those who curse you, and pray for those who abuse you.' Do you see what I mean? This war is not a holy war at all, for how can we oppose the very foundation of our faith and still claim to be righteous?"

"Tell me then, beggar, why does your army assault me in this way? If what you say is true, then there is no reason for us to fight."

"Great one, I have come to ask you to do something that would shock the leaders of my church, but I feel it is the only way to end this terrible war. I am asking you to be a better Christian than they, to inhale the true teachings of my master and let them reveal the place within you that understands peace. Perhaps if they see you living this truth it will inspire them to do the same."

Francis took a deep breath and waited for a response. The Sultan, in the meantime, could not believe his ears. He was being asked to become a better Christian than the Christians? He tried to wrap his mind around the idea, but it was so ludicrous, so insane, that he burst out laughing. Then as quickly as it began, he became silent again and looked deep into Francis' eyes.

"Tell me, beggar, why should I spare your life? You come to my court and hypnotize me with your simple words, then expect me to convert to your faith. Your eyes compel me, but it will take more than that to convince me to lay down my sword."

Suddenly Francis was filled by the spirit of the Beloved and fell to his knees. He then closed his eyes and raised his hands above his head and began praying in a loud voice.

"Oh, Lord, make me an instrument of your peace.
Where there is hatred, let me bring love.
Where there is injury, pardon.
Where there is doubt, faith.
Where there is despair, hope.
Where there is darkness, light.
Where there is sadness, joy.

Oh, Divine Master,
Grant that I may not so much seek
To be consoled as to console,
To be understood as to understand,
To be loved as to love.
For it is in giving that we receive,
It is in pardoning that we are pardoned,
And it is in dying to ourselves that we are born to
    eternal life."

Leo was not sure if he breathed at all during the prayer, but the thought of air seemed to bring him back to his body, and he filled his lungs the same instant his eyes filled with tears. Every prayer he had learned on their journey came together, and he suddenly understood the true meaning of peace, not with his mind but with his whole Self. When he looked at the Sultan, Leo knew he was experiencing a similar feeling. His eyes were closed and his head was tilted back, ever so slightly, giving the impression that he was lost in ecstasy. Then Francis stood up and walked directly to the Sultan, and when the royal guards stepped forward to intervene, the great leader opened his eyes and motioned for them to step back.

"Great king," Francis said, "that is the only thing I came to say to you. I have discovered how simple the truth is, and I thought that, if you were to understand as I, then our people could live in peace. I beg you to excuse my presumption, but the Light I see is so bright, and I so wanted you to see it as well."

The Sultan stood up and walked over to Francis, then wrapped his strong arms around the friar and began to weep. Leo watched this scene with utter amazement, as did everyone in the huge room. Then the Sultan stepped back, wiped his eyes and spoke.

"You are a magician just as my advisor claimed," he said. "And the spell you have cast has built a bridge between two great oceans—my mind and my heart. You, in your simplicity, have shown me the vanity of my life, and I suddenly remember the song I sang when I was young which bade me to love all creatures in this world. But then everything changed and I threw myself into this war, forgetting the magic of love and tolerance. Your Master is very wise indeed, little man, and I would do well to imitate his words."

"Will you then end this war and promote the peace you feel within you now?" Francis asked.

"I will try," the Sultan said. "War is a complicated issue and requires much thought and prayer. But I promise I will try, and when my people ask about the sudden change in attitude, I will say that an Italian beggar spoke a few words that changed my life. Yes, that is what I will say when they ask."

By then Leo was standing at Francis' side and the Sultan smiled at them both. "And as far as your sentence, I pardon you now, just as you have pardoned me. There is no greater gift I can give but that which I have received. That is what I learned today, and I praise Allah for this insight."

The Sultan bid Francis and Leo to stay with him as long as they chose, but the friars knew that the other brothers and sisters of their order would be waiting for them. And so they thanked the Sultan for his gift, then turned and left, beginning the long journey home.

Chapter Fifteen

"It is in dying to self that we are born to eternal life"

ays had passed yet the glow they felt from their encounter with the Sultan did not dissipate at all. Francis and Leo met many people on the road as they made their slow journey back to Assisi, both Christian and Muslim alike, and everyone seemed to feel the shift, as if the Sultan was keeping his promise and the great Crusade was about to end. Francis' joy was complete for he had accomplished his great mission regardless of the result. The chance to stand in front of the Sultan and tell him of the real message of Jesus was enough for him. The rest was in the hands of his Beloved.

Francis looked over at Leo and realized he was carrying his sketch pad beneath his arm, outside his habit. This struck him as strange since it was Leo's custom to keep the pad beneath the tunic, sheltered from the wind and rain. At first Francis didn't say a word about this change, but the question pulled at him until he could no longer remain silent.

"Brother Leo, I have noticed you carrying your pad outside your habit today, and I realized that this is not your usual practice. Tell me, has something changed that you now feel free to expose it to the open air?"

"Only one thing has changed," Leo said to him. "I have finished the portrait. We have traveled together for weeks and I have learned so many lessons from you. And now, through the grace of God, it seems that all these lessons have made their way to the page where I drew your face, and upon that page a miracle has occurred, one which I am longing to share with you."

Francis became visibly excited and said: "Oh please, Leo, tell me about this miracle, for it will mean so much more to me than a drawing of my face."

"I will tell you," Leo said, "but first I must ask you a question. When we were in front of the Sultan and you took all the lessons you gave me, weaving them together into a simple prayer, there was one line which struck a chord within me."

"Which line was that, Brother?"

"It was the final line: 'It is in dying to self that we are born to eternal life.' I have been thinking about this line for many days now, and it has led me to a very profound understanding of peace. Everything you have taught me has led to this one experience, the understanding that we must die to the definition we have of ourselves in order to remember who we really are. When we release this idea, this concept that has no relation to reality at all, then we discover the truth within, and that truth, being like a birth, sets us free."

"Brother Leo, I am overjoyed that God has inspired this understanding. You have surely accomplished your goal of realizing the peace that surpasses understanding."

"I have done it by watching you," Leo said to Francis. "Your life has taught me more than all your words, for it is in this demonstration that I entered an experience that words can never describe. As I observe the way you live your life, I come to understand the goal that motivates you more than any other. Your goal is to dissolve into the ocean of holiness and to become the Beloved. In this way all separation disappears and you perceive the altar of God where it truly is—within yourself. You do not try to be like Jesus, for then you are still separated from the one you love. Your real goal is to 'become' Christ, and in doing so to see everything through the eyes of Christ. Only then will the illusion of separation disappear, to be replaced forever by the Light that knows no shadow."

Francis did not say a word, but continued walking with his eyes cast toward the ground. Leo understood what he felt, for Francis would never go so far as to reveal this, his most secret desire. He was the essence of humility, and it was this, perhaps more than anything, that brought him to the heart of Christ.

His single desire had always been to imitate Jesus as much as was humanly possible. But then something shifted within him, a gentle prodding that gave birth to a whole new experience, that of being one with Jesus, within his heart, beating together in perfect rhythm. Francis understood all these things, but he would never say it out loud.

"And so, this portrait you have drawn of me, does it reflect this Light you have seen, Brother Leo?"

"I believe this portrait is the very essence of your prayer, Francis. Everything I have learned about peace, especially this final lesson, has been channeled into this drawing. You have taught me what it means to die to the idea of self, and to accept the reality of the Perfect Self which God perceives. This is all I see in you, my brother, and because giving and receiving are one in truth, I see it in myself. This is the greatest gift I could ever hope to achieve."

"Show me, then, this portrait that is the result of such great insight," Francis said. "Your words have convinced me that your drawing has greater value than the one who posed. Perhaps others will see the image and feel the lessons you have learned, gleaning from this portrait the very essence of the peace we seek."

Leo took the pad from beneath his arm and showed Francis the portrait he had drawn. It seemed as if the wind stopped blowing and the birds in the trees held silent as he looked. The whole world was still as Francis gazed into the eyes of this perfect face, for it was not his face at all, but the face of his Beloved, **Jesus**."

"This is what I learned," Leo said, "to look past what the physical eyes behold and see only the face of Christ. You have disappeared from my sight forever and have been replaced by the vision of holiness that was our great Master. I look into your eyes and I see Jesus, as if he were with me now. And so he is, for the face of Christ is the truth in all of us, and when we seek this truth above all things, then it is all we will ever see."

Francis began to cry, for he knew Leo had learned the true meaning of peace. Then he wiped his eyes, put his hand on Leo's shoulder and said: "Let's go home, Leo. Our brothers are waiting for us."